/23

The Sky Is Not a Ceiling

The Sky Is Not a Ceiling

An Astronomer's Faith

Aileen O'Donoghue

ORBIS BOOKS

Maryknoll, New York 10545

Library of Congress Cataloging-in-Publication Data

O'Donoghue, Aileen.
    The sky is not a ceiling : an astronomer's faith / Aileen O'Donoghue.
      p. cm.
    ISBN 978-1-57075-703-7
    1. O'Donoghue, Aileen – Religion. 2. Spiritual biography. 3. Religion and science. 4. Astronomers – Religious life. 5. Astronomers – United States – Biography. I. Title.
    QB36.O36A3 2007
    282.092 – dc22
    [B]
                                              2007014785

To

my parents, Irene and Ed,
for giving me life, love, and freedom,

my sisters, Kate and Peggy,
for giving me dreams, ambition, and unflagging support,

my brothers, John, Gerry, and Pat,
for giving me courage, tenacity, and humor,

Dave Clark,
for showing me the universe and math,

Tom Clarke,
for inviting and welcoming me into the great tradition,

and QB,
for loving me, dancing when she saw me,
and teaching me to trust again.

Contents

Acknowledgments

THIS BOOK BEGAN to emerge from fantasy in Concordia, Kansas, thanks to the courage of Sister Bette Moslander and the staff of Manna House. I connected to the Sisters of St. Joseph of Concordia through Sister Rosie Farrell, who had become one of my dear friends in Socorro while I was in graduate school. I had visited the community, stayed at Manna House, and gotten to know many of the sisters, including Bette. She recalls that I told her that I wanted to give a retreat sometime, and she'd promised to give me the opportunity. I have forgotten that exchange, but Bette risked "buying a pig in a poke" to keep her promise.

I spent a week of May 2002 creating and leading a retreat on "Loving the Universe," which included much of the material in this book. Bette, the staff of Manna House, and the retreatants all received what I had to say with an openness and eagerness that floored me. Bette told me toward the end that I had something worthwhile to say and a responsibility to say it. To help with this, they invited me back to give the retreat again in 2004.

One of the Manna House staff had a sister at Mount St. Scholastica Monastery in Atchison, Kansas. Through her and Sister Jo Ann Fellin, I was invited to give the Mary L. Fellin Lecture at Benedictine College in 2004. Through that, an editor at the *National Catholic Reporter* decided to feature me in their Faith at Large series.

Renée LaReau was sent in September of 2005 to write a feature on me.[1] As she was leaving, I handed her some of my essays. She was

---

1. René LaReau, "Sacred Starry Night," *National Catholic Reporter,* October 28, 2005.

very enthusiastic about my writing and quickly got me in touch with Mike Leach at Orbis Books. The result is this book.

I am deeply indebted to these individuals and others too numerous to name for supporting me in my seeking, struggles, profession, and writing. To all of them I offer my heartfelt gratitude and prayers.

Introduction

THROUGH MY TWENTIES, I attended the weekday morning Spanish Mass at San Miguel parish in Socorro, New Mexico. I was a Ph.D. student in physics, the youngest in the congregation by almost twenty-five years, and didn't speak Spanish. Sometimes I would look around and wonder what kind of a nut I was to be so out of step with my peers.

I still wonder what kind of a nut I am, and this book is the fruit of my trying to figure that out. It is not so much about answers as it is about making friends with the questions that drove me to both my Ph.D. work and morning Mass.

As a child I had little interest in either science or religion, though I did love nature. I was most at home perched in the branches of trees or climbing among the sun-warmed rocks of the mountains in my native Colorado. Nature was more than a "what" to me, it was a "who." I had a deep sense of a relationship with nature and a deep trust in it. I found school tolerable, but mostly uninteresting. The science classes were among the least interesting as they seemed to be mostly about measuring seemingly senseless quantities and following tedious instructions instead of the world outside my window that I loved. It wasn't until an earth science professor at Colorado Mountain College threw open the curtains on the universe that I connected the academic disciplines of science to nature. Once I did, my life path among the academics emerged to the consternation and amazement of myself and all who knew me.

I attended Mass and catechism classes (as our Catholic "Sunday school" was called), and religion was a part of my life, but like school, it was tolerable but uninteresting. I was always aware of contradictions about the life of Jesus in the three synoptic Gospels and aware that little of what was said in the context of religion and Mass seemed to have an impact on real life. This awareness sharpened for me by being part of the parish at Fitzsimons army hospital during the Vietnam war. Among the parishioners at Mass there were often wounded soldiers. I still see the bandaged young men in beds and wheel chairs when I think back to Mass at Fitz. My parents required me to attend catechism classes until I finished the sixth grade — not an uncommon ending point for Catholic religious studies for those who don't attend Catholic schools. They required that I attend Mass until I moved out of their house. On my own initiative, I chose to get confirmed at seventeen. I went through the classes and did the reading but still found the contradictions. Though I was confirmed, I gave up on finding anything meaningful in religion, stopped attending Mass as soon as I could, and wasn't sure if I believed in God. I certainly didn't believe in the "Great White Father" God keeping score on sins that I had learned of in my Catholic experience.

As my Catholic experience faded from importance in my life, my studies in science led me to an understanding of the origins of the universe that did not require God. Hence I found myself an atheist. Intellectually, it seemed the most honest approach to the universe and the approach required of one aspiring to a career in science. What I didn't realize was that the benevolent "who-ness" of nature in which I'd always felt a sense of trust had gotten twisted up with the God of my Catholic childhood. When I lost my intellectual belief in God, I also lost my sense of personal connection with nature and the universe.

This crystallized for me one winter night as an undergraduate at Fort Lewis College when I stood in the snow looking up at a star-filled sky and saw only stars. I realized that previously I had seen a sort of ceiling like a transparent blanket with which benevolent nature protected me. The sky was a sort of roof beyond which God was overseeing the world and protecting holy people as it promises in Psalm 91: "You who dwell in the shelter of the Most High, who abide in the shadow of the Almighty — God commands the angels to guard you in all your ways. With their hands they shall support you, lest you strike your foot against a stone" (Ps. 91:1, 9, 11–12). That night I gazed into an emptiness that I couldn't have previously imagined. It remains the most mystical experience that I have ever had, and as I looked into the depths of the sky, the chill of the winter night sank into the core of my being.

Actually, the chill had begun to seep into my soul, and a crack had begun to open in the ceiling of the sky seven years earlier when a friend and I were sexually assaulted at a library less than a block from our homes. I had had complete trust in my world until then. God and the universe would not let anything bad happen to me. Feeling the muzzle of a gun against my temple on a random Tuesday night let me know that bad things could, indeed, happen to me, and the fear I felt that night would remain a close companion for decades.

Though I had a deep sense of betrayal by the universe after that, I associated it with humans and cities, holding my trust in nature apart and sacred. I knew that people could murder me, but I clung to a sense of nature's benevolence that wouldn't let me fall from my perch in the trees. But when I looked up at the sky that night at Fort Lewis, a sense of empty indifference replaced my sense of benevolence. Nature didn't care if I fell. Nature didn't have the least care about me. It didn't care if I was good or bad, hurt or well. It didn't matter that I even existed. Suddenly the star-filled sky was bereft of a love I hadn't consciously realized I clung to. My sense of loss was profound. The universe was empty, and I was profoundly alone inside my skin. The physical chill of that night seemed to last for months. It wasn't until the following August while sitting on the steps of the Art Institute of Chicago during a visit to my sister that I realized I could again feel the warmth of the sun. But the chill of loneliness in my soul persisted and, much to my consternation and amazement, eventually drove me to the morning Spanish Mass at San Miguel parish.

The path from my winter night of the soul to the morning Mass was cold, lonely, and frightening. And it was not a magic pill. Morning Mass did not end with "she lived happily ever after."

Once I found myself as a Ph.D. student in physics at the morning Mass, I had to put these two worlds together within myself. Initially I felt like a fraud in both worlds. I was a fraud as a scientist because I needed to believe in God. It felt as though I imposed God on the universe to assuage my loneliness and that was a very unscientific thing to do. As a Catholic, my fraudulence lurked in the fact that I still saw all the contradictions and questioned Catholic doctrine and church structures with the mind of a scientist. There were other scientists I knew who belonged to churches. Some were even Catholic. When I talked with them about living in two worlds, I found that, for the most part, they neatly compartmentalized their scientific and religious selves, accepting them as being in different realms with little or no common intersection. But I was the living intersection and was not satisfied with compartmentalization. I felt like a person standing on two icebergs trying desperately not to be ripped apart by their separate motions on the sea of life. I am still trying, though I am much better at it than I was in graduate school. I have brought them close enough to touch and even temporarily bind, but they are still not completely fused. I doubt they ever will be.

So what can I hope to contribute by writing about my life in two worlds? Well, I believe that in the current national discussions about science and religion, my journey from uninterest to fraudulence to integration may express a point of view rarely expressed and ideas rarely voiced. They include:

- that science and religion are not mutually exclusive,

- that what we've learned about the universe through our scientific methods is a delight to both the mind and the soul,

- that such a universe points to a God much weirder and elusive than any of our religions describe or preach, and

- that it is possible to find a resting place among the stars and vast stretches of intergalactic space as comfortable as one among the branches of a favorite tree or the rocks of a favorite mountain.

Chapter 1

Wonder Bread and the Game Show God

AMONG MY MEMORIES from elementary school is a field trip where I was mesmerized by the production line in the Wonder Bread bakery. The loaves of bread rode on tracks through an incredible series of machines that sliced them, bagged them, and dropped them into plastic cases to be stacked into trucks and driven, fresh, to grocery stores all over the Mile-High City. Perhaps my fascination was one of the early signs of the geekery that would blossom in me a decade later. But at that time it was simply fascination and delight with things that are neat, well-ordered, and efficient. I still like such things, delighting in the view of urban highways from airplanes, though I know now to distrust such neatness and efficiency in human affairs.

The Wonder Bread bakery's impact still resonates with me for two reasons. The first is that I've been teaching physics for more than two decades and would love for my students to see and respond to such beautiful efficiency. The second is that Wonder Bread is a telling icon of my childhood years. It was billed to "build strong bodies 12 ways" due to flour enriched with vitamins and minerals. The current website claims this was part of a "quiet miracle" in nutrition that almost eliminated diseases such as beriberi and pellagra linked to vitamin deficiencies. Yet I found Wonder Bread to be little more substantial than cotton candy. Maybe I just don't have the taste for white bread. I never did comprehend people who tear the crusts off their bread since the crust has the most substance. Nevertheless, the icon of Wonder Bread that is wedded to my memories of the late 1960s and early 1970s is one of uniformity and hollow promises.

I was born in Denver, Colorado, in 1958 and grew up in Aurora, a suburb to its east. It was a white bread world with very few people of color or local ethnicity. It was the white, suburban America of Beaver Cleaver, and yet there was a dark side that the Cleavers never acknowledged. That dark side was the hollowness of the promise of nutrition that melts away like cotton candy, the promise of "liberty and justice for all" that sent the children of the poor to suffer and die in southeast Asia while the children of privilege and connections joined protests against the draft with their deferments carefully tucked away, and the promise of *Saturn V* rockets launching men on journeys to the moon even as the dread of rockets bringing nuclear annihilation lurked in all our hearts.

Cold and Hot Wars

Both the Cold War and the hot war in Vietnam (that, we were often reminded, was not a war since Congress had not declared it) were constant presences in my life. We were told in school that the "bombs could drop at any moment," and we all speculated about how life would change "when the Russians invaded." It didn't produce an active fear in us, but more a cold, dark dread that we were living on borrowed time and the world we knew was doomed to destruction. I still carry that dread, though I now attribute it to my awareness of how precariously our society and lifestyle are perched on unsustainable energy, economic, and agricultural processes.

For me, the active fear was of the fate of my brothers in Vietnam. The evening news usually led with casualty counts, and soldiers were always at Mass at our army parish. My oldest brother enlisted in the navy when I was nine, in 1967. My second brother followed two years later. My youngest brother (still five years my senior) was considering defection to Canada the night the birthday lottery reprieved him with a draw of 362.[2] Though my older brothers enlisted for six-year stints with the submarine corps to avoid Vietnam, I didn't quite trust that they wouldn't end up like the wounded soldiers at Mass or under one of the countless white crosses at Fort Logan National Cemetery, which we drove by on our way to the mountains for picnics.

I was haunted through those years by a dream I had early in my oldest brother's enlistment. My dream began with a box from the Navy arriving at our house. When we opened it, it was filled with chips resembling the broken shards of a fresh coconut with the white coconut meat lining the inside. But it wasn't a coconut, it was my brother's skull and the meat was what was left of his brains. I awoke from that dream with a fear I would carry until the last troops left the roof of the embassy in Saigon. It reawakens every time I watch another generation going off to yet another war, leaving little sisters to worry and cry themselves to sleep.

Religion in Aurora

Religion was mostly a sideline event in the lives of us neighborhood kids. It was regular, our trooping off to our respective churches every Sunday, but not particularly meaningful. As a Catholic kid, I also trooped off on Saturday mornings for catechism class while my Protestant pals were happily playing. With only an hour in Mass the next morning, I played alone while all my friends attended Sunday school. I knew only one Jew, with whom I wasn't very close, and didn't know what day of the weekend was her sacrifice to religion. I did know that she traded in Christmas for Chanukkah, and I wasn't sure if it was a gain or a loss, given the rumors of eight days of presents! I didn't know any Muslims, Hindus, or Buddhists, though the Hare Krishna cult members did appear in the airport concourses chanting and begging in my preteen years. The different hours when we had to sacrifice our play for religion were the only differences among the

---

2. To prioritize men for the draft, the dates of the year were drawn by lottery and men drafted in order of their birth dates.

faiths that we understood. When we compared notes, we discovered that each of our religions claimed to be the "one true faith." As for us, children who could sing the jingles of just about every product advertised on TV, we took these claims as seriously as we took claims of being better than "brand X."

In our TV-informed universe, religion seemed much like a cosmic *Let's Make a Deal*, where contestants traded some odd object or costume they had brought from home for what was behind various numbered doors. Some of the doors hid wonderful prizes such as cars and vacation packages. Others held gag prizes such as a cow wearing sunglasses and a feather boa. Throughout the show, Monty Hall offered money for odd items and for a bid for taking whatever was behind a door or curtain. It seemed to me that in the cosmic *Let's Make a Deal,* each religion claimed that God was behind their door with the great dinner party of heaven (that sounded quite dull to our childish minds) and behind all the other doors lurked fire, brimstone, and eternal damnation. God's enemy, the Devil, wandered about offering riches and promises to coax people away from the "One True Door" to one of the doomed doors. Needless to say, we didn't take the claims of truth of our religions very seriously.

Looking back, I envision the *Let's Make a Deal* set with each religion gathered in front of its own door waiting for God to be revealed. The Protestants gather in front of door number three, seated around folding tables and passing covered dishes of string beans in cream of mushroom soup. The Catholics are in front of door number two with nuns and a few old people kneeling in neat rows reciting the rosary with the speed of a horse-race announcer. The priests gather in the front in strict hierarchical order and a few of the Knights (of Columbus) hang out at the back bar drinking beer. At door number one are the Jews; men in black hats and long coats standing at the door rocking in their prayers and wedging little notes into gaps between the panels. In the back, a Klezmer band plays, and a few men and women in uniforms wander about with their Uzis. At a second door number two (confusing the Catholics) rows of Muslim men kneel shoulder to shoulder on their prayer mats, bowing their heads to the floor while old women in head scarves and burkas watch from the back. Along the boundary with door number one, the young Jewish and Muslim men stand face to face arguing about the exact placement of the line. The Buddhists and Hindus don't bother with the doors and are off in the park chanting and circumambulating the hall. The Unitarian Universalists, also certain that God doesn't lurk behind any of the doors, are in the parking lot hoping to get out before the rush when everyone else discovered that truth. The women of the Catholics, Jews, and Muslims are mostly in the basement preparing meals and running after the kids so they don't disturb the men upstairs and recognizing that the reality of their lives is fairly independent of their religion.

This was as seriously as I took religion, and it expresses the nonsense I saw in it. I was told that only Catholics got into heaven and my Protestant friends were told Catholics couldn't get into heaven. But all of us were taught that non-Christians certainly couldn't get into heaven and that the purpose of life was to get into heaven. That puzzled me a great deal since I imagined that non-Christian people were probably a lot like us and were probably not Christian because of where they grew up, just as I was Christian because of my family. Would the God who they always said loved us really condemn people for believing their family's religion? Very much like *Let's Make a Deal*, it seemed like a cosmic guessing game, and even as a child I found that a rather absurd expression of a loving God.

Actually, I wasn't sure about how loving God really was. The God I understood from church was a Great White Father in the sky who kept careful track of how many impure thoughts I had, how many bad words I said, and wouldn't like me at all if it hadn't been for Jesus, though I didn't have a clue what I could have done to offend God so deeply. I just didn't buy the idea of original sin. My parents got over it fairly quickly when I ate something they told me not to. They also managed to forgive me without beating my older brother, so why was God so hung up on an apple and why did God require Jesus to die to forgive us? In this context, the claims of God's great love rang as hollowly as my Wonder Bread icon. There's no forgiveness from God without punishment? What kind of love is that? Also, stories from the Holocaust and stories of innocent people being tortured and killed on the evening news left me puzzled as to why we were supposed to see Jesus as so special. Didn't people die all the time trying to protect the ones they loved? And they weren't God, and they didn't really know what might happen to them after death, whereas Jesus seems to have been quite certain of going to heaven. The story just didn't hold together for me and yet left me feeling vaguely guilty that I existed at all and confused as to why.

At home we didn't discuss religion, though I recall my mother helping me memorize my prayers and passing on her mother's advice to "listen to what they say, and do what you think is right." As a child I did not see my parents pray outside church, and they never referenced the Bible, homilies, or anything from church. We simply went to Mass and participated in the required sacraments. I saw much of what we did as acquiring merit badges for getting into heaven. We Catholic kids had to learn to recite all our prayers, obey all the rules, and dutifully report every infraction to the priest in confession. I recall leaving confession once, after having said my ten Our Fathers and ten Hail Marys, and thinking that my soul was all clean and as soon as I thought, spoke, or acted, I'd start dirtying it up again.

From my observations of the adults — the priests, nuns, and leaders of the parish who we were certain were going to heaven — I deduced that being kind wasn't necessarily required. Some of them seemed quite comfortable treating us kids with discourtesy and sometimes outright meanness. If they were all going to be in heaven, I wasn't so sure I wanted to go.

When my parents first moved to Aurora and were involved with their geographically determined parish, they had a terrible experience with a priest, which drove them to join the parish at Fitzsimons army hospital. I have learned little of what happened since it occurred before my birth, but it resulted in all my Catholic experience taking place at Fitz and all my sacramental records being held by the Department of the Army. There was a chapel that served all active faiths on the post where we most often went to Mass. Due to sharing the space, however, the 8:00 a.m. Sunday morning Mass was at Bushnell auditorium on the eighth floor of the hospital, where President Dwight Eisenhower had recovered from a heart attack in 1955 and the presidential candidate John Kerry had been born in 1943. When we went to Mass there, I was struck by the magnificent view of the snow-capped peaks of the Rocky Mountains from the windows and the presence of soldiers wounded in Vietnam.

In religion classes, I tended to keep quiet and do what I was told, waiting for it to mean something. I had questions that I felt I could never ask, though I'm not sure why I felt that way. The silliest of them was the meaning of Christ. Was it Jesus' last name? For years I wondered about this, not figuring it out until some time in high school. I also wondered why Mary and Joseph, after losing the twelve-year-old Jesus in Jerusalem, were confused by his telling them that he had to be about his Father's business. . . . Didn't they remember Mary's angel, Joseph's dream, the shepherds and the Wise Men? They supposedly knew he was the son of God at his conception. Did they forget that by the time he was twelve? When Jesus and John the Baptist met at the Jordan river, why didn't they know each other; weren't they cousins. Hadn't Mary visited John's mom, Elizabeth, when they were both pregnant? Was that the only visit? My cousins visited us in Colorado from Massachusetts, Alabama, and Washington state more than once while I was a kid and they were a lot further away than Mary was from Elizabeth. These things still confuse me when people claim that everything in the Gospels is literally true. It just doesn't fit, and it puzzles me that others don't seem to see that.

There were also the more troubling disconnects between what Jesus said we should do and what we actually did. Jesus said to call no one on earth father because there was only one Father, so why did we call all the priests Father? Jesus said to love our enemies, and yet the soldiers at Mass, the whole and the wounded, testified that we were still busy hating and killing our enemies. Jesus said if someone demands your cloak, give him your coat as well, and yet complaints about "welfare queens" abounded.

Then there was the church's devaluation of women. We girls felt it sharply as the call for boys to be altar servers went out every year. I don't know if I would have been a server, but being excluded from even trying because of how I was on the outside, without the least interest in what I was like on the inside angered me. They did always say that our outer appearance was not as important as the condition of our soul. So why did gender matter so much? The church just didn't seem to *see* women. They said women weren't at the last supper so they weren't "ordained" by Jesus, yet they had been everywhere else with Jesus, and I couldn't imagine the men cooking and serving themselves. Also, if Mary Magdalene was the first person Jesus appeared to after he rose, why wasn't she an apostle while Paul, who'd never met Jesus in life, was?

These and many more questions were the sort of thing that confused us kids and made religion seem like a bit of a fairy story with aspects as incomprehensible as spinning flax into gold and wolves dressed as grandmothers. Yet we were supposed to *believe* everything in religion. We did discuss these questions among ourselves and some were more bothered than others, but none of us were certain that the grown-ups really knew what they were talking about. After all, by the time we were twelve, Santa Claus, the Easter Bunny, and the Tooth Fairy had all been revealed as unreal, and in many ways Jesus didn't seem terribly different.

Perhaps if I had lived in a more ethnic neighborhood where everyone was Catholic or if I had gone to Catholic school, I would have found religion more real. My only contact with the local Catholic school was getting beaten up in the playground of Peoria public school by a bunch of kids from St. Therese. Among my university colleagues, the women who went to Catholic school and have mostly left the church claim that not attending Catholic school may have been the salvation of my faith.

It has always struck me that the Catholic schools educated a lot of kids right out of the church by developing their minds and then expecting them to be checked at the church door. This is illustrated by an incident from Karen Armstrong's experience of the novitiate at a convent where she was assigned an essay to "assess the quality of the evidence for the resurrection." She read all the required books and thought deeply about the arguments put forth and found she just didn't believe them. It wasn't logical; one couldn't "prove" the resurrection from the incidents in the Gospels. But she knew she had to write for the exam, so she "reproduced the mental gymnastics"[3] of proving that there was sufficient evidence in the Gospels for anyone who read them to believe that Jesus was divine and had risen from the dead. She felt a loss of integrity in writing it, but the nun to whom she turned it in acclaimed it as excellent. In response, Karen asked "It just isn't true, what I've written, is it?" To which the nun responded "No, Sister. No, it isn't true, but please don't tell the other novices."[4] There are those in the church like "the other novices" who believe the "mental sleights of hand"[5] from the apologetics, but I also know many very intelligent and well-educated people in the church who see the untruths and mental gymnastics and have simply chosen to live with them as the inevitable creations of an institution and not the essence of the faith. It is now what I have chosen to do, but it is a constant challenge to not let them drive me away from the practice of any religion as they finally did Karen Armstrong.

I did give the church a serious try when I was seventeen and decided on my own to seek Confirmation. My parents expressed no concern about whether or not I chose to be confirmed. By that time, my five siblings had been confirmed, ranging in age from twenty-two to thirty, and had left the church. I assume my parents didn't think Confirmation made much of a difference. Hence of my own free will,

---

3. Karen Armstrong, *Through the Narrow Gate* (New York: St. Martin's Press, 1981), 154.
4. Ibid., 155.
5. Ibid.

wondering if I hadn't missed something people were trying to tell me in religious classes, I attended the classes and made the retreat necessary to be confirmed. Our retreat was at Camp St. Malo in a picturesque valley just west of Denver. I delighted in the mountains and silence. And I spent long periods in the chapel seeking whatever it was that was supposed to move me there. Nothing did, though the scent of the pines in the rain and the sun glinting off the pond filled me with comforting sense that there was a "who-ness" to the universe with whom I had a relationship of love. I didn't think of this as the God they told me about in church and left the retreat thinking that I didn't know how to pray or was somehow inadequate as a Catholic. I did get confirmed and, much to my surprise, my parents actually had a bit of a party for me with cake and ice cream. Later that year, though, as I left my parents' home for college, I left Catholicism there in a drawer with my confirmation certificate.

Chapter 2

When the Universe Betrayed Me

I T WAS DECEMBER 20, 1972. I was fourteen years old and my parents were having a Christmas party. My friend and I headed the half-block down to the local public library to do some homework. We worked for an hour or two and were heading home about 8:00 p.m. We stopped in the strip of park beside the library and sat on a concrete power access box to have a smoke together before going to our separate homes. As we sat in the semi-dark smoking and talking, a man walked up.

He seemed young. Perhaps a new soldier from the nearby army base. He asked us directions to a major street, which we supplied, disagreeing on the most direct route. Then he pulled out a sawed-off shotgun and said, "I have a better idea. Pull up your shirts." Even now, more than thirty years later, I can still feel the jolt of adrenaline that shot through me at the sight of that gun. My breath caught and my head spun into a sense of unreality, a refusal to believe what was happening. This couldn't happen in Aurora! This couldn't happen to me!

The man fondled our breasts, then made us lie down in the snow and open our pants. He fondled us more, kissing and licking our pubic areas. He seemed very nervous himself, as though he'd never done this before. After threatening to rape my friend, who pleaded with him not to, he made her suck his penis. Neither of us had a clue what fellatio was, but we learned that night. He switched over to me. The barrel of his gun pushed against my head as he pumped his penis in my mouth. After an eternity of fear, disgust, and discomfort, he ejaculated. I spit out his semen and wished I could throw up. He told us to leave, going the long way out of the park. We walked away from him, the aim of his gun prickling the backs of our necks. Once we turned the corner, we ran home, tears of terror streaming down our faces. We could have been killed! My house was half a block from the library, my friend's half a block farther. We didn't say anything to each other.

I got home terrified and disgusted and ran through the living room full of party guests to my bedroom where I told my story. My older sister stayed with me, my brothers and brother-in-law went out hunting for the guy with knives (and, fortunately, didn't find him), my parents had to be polite to their guests knowing I was traumatized. It was the 1970s when many (particularly among the police) still blamed girls and women for getting raped, not the men who raped them.

The police were called and came to get my story, but were more interested in whether I was drinking my coke straight or spiked. They weren't much help. The man was never caught, as far as I know.

Now we'd name what I went through after my assault PTSD, but in those days I was told to put it out of my mind and get on with my life. After all, he didn't do me any real harm. But the terror would not leave me for twenty-five years. Every man was a threat to me and every situation dangerous. I felt betrayed by the universe, by the darkness in which I had always felt safe. All in an evening I learned that I could die in the darkness for no better reason than being a female when a predatory male happened by. I hated my body for being female. When I went to the bathroom I wished I could cut my body off and flush it down the toilet or at least rip out my female organs. They were dirty; they were disgusting. They could get me killed. When I saw my friend next, she said that since I reminded her of what happened, she didn't want to be friends anymore. I had few other friends. I plunged into the first of many deep depressions, hating myself, terrified of everything, and convinced that suicide was the only way to stop feeling so awful. The only way to stop being me. But I couldn't do that to my mom.

After over thirty years, that deep wound has mostly healed, though there will always be a tenderness there, a threat of reinfection. To cope with my terror I developed a spirituality. In a thirty-day silent retreat thirty years later, I finally came to peace with the betrayal. I am again at home in the dark. I've had loving sexual encounters and no longer associate sex with death, though fellatio leaves me cold. I no longer hate myself. In fact, at this point, I rather like myself, female organs and all. In this I have to admit that the immensity of that event and my response to it shaped me into this person that I now like and whom others like and even admire. I can't hate that it happened to me. But I can hate that it happens anew to another person every hour of every day. It is for the new victims that I now weep.

Chapter 3

Waking Up to the Universe

AFTER HIGH SCHOOL, I only wanted to get a job that would support me well enough to get my own apartment. The economy of 1976 didn't cooperate. Only a few years after the first oil crisis, there were few jobs for unskilled, uneducated kids of the suburbs. The boys could get construction or other well-paying jobs, but competition was fierce among us girls for the few grocery store jobs that paid enough to live on. I didn't make the cut. So, in the defeat of unemployment, I decided to go to college.

Going to college had always been an option for me, but my boredom at school had made me ambivalent to the entire academic enterprise. There was certainly an intellectual tone to family life. My father had gotten his degree at Holy Cross College after World War II and books abounded in our house. Though they didn't push any of us to go to college, my parents let us know it was a valuable thing to do, and they would help all they could to get us through.

Just after I turned five, my sister Kate had entered the University of Colorado to study engineering. It made me famous among other first-graders to have a sister in college, and I was very proud. Kate was very successful at CU, where she served as the first female editor of the *Colorado Engineer* magazine and was featured on a Denver television program. Three years later, Peggy followed Kate to CU, where she began a math major. Moving to San Francisco, Peggy was hired by the Bank of America and had advanced to a vice president by the time I was in high school. Also when I was in high school, Kate went on to earn her M.B.A. in finance. Thus when I did decide to attend college, majoring in engineering, math, business or, as it turned out, science, was quite possible because my sisters had done it before me. They also encouraged me to keep my options open for college while I was in high school and supported me intellectually, emotionally, and sometimes financially on my long academic journey. I am forever in their debt.

Once I decided to go to college, choosing one was quite simple. I marvel at stories of kids and parents sweating college applications and taking a week to travel to different schools. I had left high school with the very minimum to graduate so I was not overwhelmed with choices. Having looked at the snow-capped peaks of the Rocky Mountains across the city of Denver from my parents' front windows, one thing I was certain of was that I wanted a college in the midst of those mountains.

Throughout my adolescence, I had longed for wilderness and dreamed of homesteading in the wilderness of the Yukon Territory. Each time I was able to get into the mountains, usually when relatives from distant states visited, it was an opportunity to journey in my mind to a place far from my suburban stresses to a world where things were simpler and the stresses more basic and meaningful: food, shelter, warmth. Every summer during high school, I applied for the Youth Conservation Corps, but was never selected. The only opportunity I had to learn about life on and with the land was the Vocational Agriculture program through my high school. Looking back, having access to "the farm" was an important part of my surviving high school. Each morning for my three years of high school (ninth grade was in "junior high" in those days), we few Ag students would ride the bus from our high school to the farm.

It wasn't instruction on the farm that made the difference to me; it was simply being there and being involved with the animals and shop. As a public school farm in the midst of suburban Denver, we often had elementary school groups visit to see the animals. Leading them around the farm and describing the different animals, I discovered that I really enjoyed it and wondered if I could some day make a living as a tour guide. In many ways, that's exactly what I am!

In my junior year, I raised a lamb, whom I named Shagnasticus after my friend's cat Shagnasty. I learned how to show sheep in preparation for the National Western Stock Show, at one point winning a sixth place ribbon in a field of seven! I had no illusion about my future in showmanship. I joined the Future Farmers of America (FFA) and managed to become a "Chapter Farmer" that same year. That was the complete extent of my involvement in high school clubs. At the National Western, the building where the animals were kept and the large rodeo arena were on opposite sides of I-70, connected by a concrete tunnel under the highway. Our FFA group contracted to sweep the underpass daily so I spent many hours at the stock show, sometimes catching a nap in the fresh straw with the sheep. Neither my little sheep nor myself won any ribbons, and the Ag instructor negotiated the sale of the sheep, who simply disappeared from their pen. After feeding and working with my lamb for three months, I sold it for about what I had paid for it. I realized then that farming was not likely going to pan out for me as a way to make a living, particularly since I had no land or capital, so I turned my dreams to the wilderness.

To start on my path, I went to Colorado Mountain College (CMC) a community college outside Glenwood Springs, Colorado. My intention was to complete an associate of applied science degree in Natural Resource Management (NRM). Essentially, it was a program to learn some basic science and skills for forest service work. It was a two-year program after which I would have a credential with which I could find a job that paid a living wage and allowed me to live in the mountains. I learned some very useful things in that program, but my plan for a future in the Forest Service evaporated in my first quarter.

On my first full day at CMC, filled with meeting new people and discovering new places, I noticed a tall, thin man leading a small group of people about the campus. The fact that I remember seeing him on that first day may just be because his height set him apart, or because I found out a day later that he was Dr. Dave Clark, my earth science professor, or it may be that some part of me knew that he was going to change my life in a way that neither I nor anyone who knew me could have guessed.

Earth science was a required course for NRM. I didn't even know what it was. In high school, I had droned through a required year of biology before giving up on science out of sheer boredom. From the beginning of Dave's course, I was enthralled. Not that the lectures were multimedia extravaganzas like we have now. He simply wrote and drew on the chalkboard and by that threw open the curtains on the universe for me. There on the chalkboard were the glacier-carved mountain landscapes that had lured me across Denver to this mountain college. I couldn't get enough of the material and still have my course notes, carefully recopied after every class in multicolored inks.

In the classes, labs, and field trips, Dave taught us to read the history of Earth in the rocks. Spring Valley, where we lived and studied at CMC, was formed by lava that flowed out of cracks and fissures during a late uplift of the Rockies a million years earlier. Outside the window of the lab, glacier-sculpted Mt. Sopris soared to almost thirteen thousand feet above the valleys of the Roaring Fork and Crystal rivers. Just west of the mountain's base, silt deposits of a sea that retreated westward from the rising of the Ancestral Rocky Mountains more than 300 million years earlier, had metamorphosed into the flawless white marble quarried to build the Lincoln Memorial and Tomb of the Unknown Soldier.[6] Between CMC and Mt. Sopris, the Roaring Fork river had cut through the redbeds of the Maroon Formation formed from the erosional debris of those Ancestral Rockies.[7] For me, the very rocks came to life like words in a book, or more, like Annie Sullivan's incessant spelling of words in Helen Keller's hand

---

6. Halka Chronic, *Roadside Geology of Colorado* (Missoula, Mont.: Mountain Press, 1980), 131.
7. Ibid., 203.

in *The Miracle Worker*. I, like Helen Keller, suddenly connected with the world around me in a new and incredibly rich way.

The love for nature I had always carried surged forth, and the latent scholar who had languished through school awoke. It was as though I had been sleeping through the previous twelve years and suddenly woke up to a world of curiosity and intellectual challenge. My mind caught fire. I who had slouched through school with Bs and Cs was suddenly at the top of many of my classes. I decided to become a geologist and pursue the earth science that had woken me up.

Most of this was an intellectual awakening, but a fair bit of it was a father-figure infatuation with Dave. From that first quarter at CMC, watching him teach, I wanted to become a college professor, someone who knew about the natural world and could explain it in as simple and enthralling a way as Dave. I began a true discipleship where I clung to him like a barnacle striving to learn all he could teach me and basking in the approval so much easier to obtain than my own father's. I remain grateful for his kindness, his patience, and the gift of his example of the intellectual life.

Emulating Dave, who had a B.S. in Math and a Ph.D. in botany, meant that I had to make up for all the math and introductory science I had avoided in school. I spent every afternoon in Dave's lab with him patiently tutoring me in math. Algebra seemed at first a tedious secret code that I mastered only because it was an excuse for hanging out in Dave's lab. Trigonometry, though, delighted me with its ratios and circles. I hadn't bothered with geometry in high school, or I might have discovered this years earlier! The next year, the best possible circumstance arose as Dave Clark taught the calculus class.

The day I bought my big red calculus text, I sat on the bed in my dorm room and cried in intimidation. I wasn't smart enough to do calculus! Taking my fear to Dave, he recommended setting a time and place where I would daily study calculus. I chose the study carrel nearest his office, of course! For an entire academic year, I became a late afternoon fixture in that carrel, working through both calculus and my math anxiety with my hero and mentor mere yards away. Not only did I succeed at calculus; I excelled and delighted in it. Wow. Math! Me? I was becoming someone I could not have imagined.

I also took physics during that second year at CMC. I found the material completely opaque. Things seemed to make sense in the lectures, but all the problems read like Tom Robbins's quintessential algebra problem: "If a hen and a half can lay an egg and a half in a day and a half, how long will it take a monkey with a wooden leg to kick the seeds out of a dill pickle?"[8] And yet, when the professor went through the solutions of the problems, they made perfect sense and were quite elegant. I struggled to get a "D" and didn't sign up for a second quarter. Instead, I took everything I could from Dave Clark: a full year of calculus plus field botany and astronomy. The field botany course opened my eyes to the wildflowers as earth science had to the rocks. Hiking and driving through western Colorado and eastern Utah, I learned to spot penstemons, lupines, and mariposa lilies along the roadsides, in sweeps of grassland, and nestled in ravines. At night, we followed pathways across the sky marked by bright stars and the glitter of the Milky Way. As I lay on the desert floor on a trip to Arches National Park, I was surrounded, embraced even, by a familiar and delightful world. From the sand and rocks beneath my back, to the desert plants surrounding me to the stars and planets glittering above me, all was good and I was a part of it.

As I gazed at the stars and constellations now becoming familiar companions, I called them by names that also linked me to the long line of humanity that had gazed up at the same skies. In the spring-time sky of Arches, the winter hexagon yet lingered in the western sky. In the star names and the stories, the drama of millennia of human history lingers.

The downside of Colorado Mountain College was that it was a two-year curriculum. Though there were, of course, those hangers-on who managed to spend decades getting their associate's degree,

---

8. Tom Robbins, *Even Cowgirls Get the Blues* (New York: Bantam Books, 2003), 14.

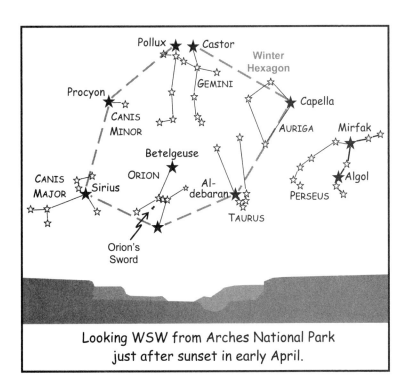

**Looking WSW from Arches National Park
just after sunset in early April.**

I had actually been launched by my experience at CMC, and for all that I loved Dave, I knew I had to move on. Not that I didn't cling!

In the summer after my graduation, I worked at CMC painting dorms for my rent and working in the cafeteria as a baker and dishwasher for a variety of groups that came to campus. It was odd to be living alone in the dorms previously filled with my friends. I had no TV or radio and only a mattress on the floor as a bed. Since I slept with the doors of the building and the room wide open, one night a squirrel digging under my mattress for a nesting site startled me awake. It was a delightful couple of months that I spent there.

An insatiable reader, I would sit outside under a lamp along the sidewalk to read. One of the books I read that summer was *The Cosmic Connection* by Carl Sagan. It inspired me to want to be an astronomer, to learn about the entire universe, not just the Earth as a geologist.

Though I had learned of stellar evolution in astronomy class, it took reading Sagan's book for it to sink in that I was as much a child of the universe as I was a child of Earth. In his chapters on the "Starfolk," he explained that the very elements we're made of, the carbon, oxygen, nitrogen, calcium, etc., were forged in the cores of stars from primordial hydrogen and helium. The heavier elements, the iron in our blood and iodine in our thyroids, could only have been forged in a supernova. Thus the stars were within me as my flesh and bone and blood. I committed the last paragraph of "Starfolk: A Fable" to memory and would find myself reciting it often when I looked up at the stars:

> And then one day there came to be a creature whose genetic material was in no major way different from the self-replicating molecular collectives of the other organisms on his planet, which he called Earth. But he was able to ponder the mystery of his origins, the strange and tortuous path by which he had emerged from star stuff. He was the matter of the cosmos, contemplating itself.... He was one of the starfolk. And he longed to return to the stars.[9]

A longing for the stars that I have yet to shake took hold. There on the CMC campus, when I left the circle of lamplight on the sidewalk, I could look up to the night sky and see the history of the elements that formed the Earth with its mountains and oceans, its sagebrush and piñon pine, the squirrel seeking a nest in my mattress and myself.

Looking to the southern sky, the constellations of Scorpius and Sagittarius glittered with the stars of the Milky Way. The asterism of the teapot in Sagittarius was easy to pick out from the glitter due to its bright stars. Above the spout of the teapot, the Lagoon

---

9. Carl Sagan, produced by Jerome Agel, *The Cosmic Connection: An Extraterrestrial Perspective* (New York: Anchor Books, 1973), 255.

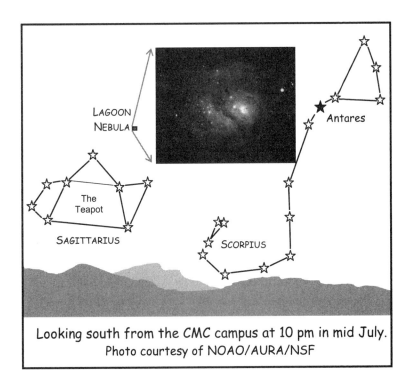

Looking south from the CMC campus at 10 pm in mid July.
Photo courtesy of NOAO/AURA/NSF

Nebula, a fuzzy blur lurked at a point making a diamond out of the triangular spout. I could see few details without the help of the campus telescope, yet I knew that smudge of light was a cloud of dust and gas one hundred light-years across. Mostly it glowed the red of hydrogen gas heated by nearby stars, but it was encircled by a dark lane that made it look like an island's lagoon. The dark lane is caused by dense gas and dust blocking light from the rest. Here small, dense globules of gas were contracting under gravity's relentless pull. As they shrink, the cores become extremely hot and dense. When the temperature reaches 10 million Kelvin, hydrogen begins fusing into helium and the globule becomes a star.

A hydrogen atom consists of one proton and one electron. A helium atom has two protons, two neutrons and two electrons. In the fusion reaction, two of the protons become neutrons by combining with electrons and binding with the remaining two protons. The resulting helium atom turns out to have slightly less mass than the original four hydrogens; 0.7 percent less to be exact. This tiny bit of mass is released as energy according to Einstein's famous equation, $E=mc^2$. Though the mass lost in a single reaction is extremely tiny, around 10^{-20} micrograms, the fact that it is multiplied by $c = 3 \times 10^8 m/s = 186,000$ miles/sec squared, makes the energy significant, about 5 trillionths of a joule.[10] Still quite small, to be sure, but in the cores of even small stars, there are many of these reactions. Our nearby star, Sol, fuses a mass of hydrogen equivalent to 62 aircraft carriers per second, converting a mass equivalent to almost half an aircraft carrier into energy. Multiply that mass, around a hundred metric tons, by the speed of light squared and you get enough energy for fifty billionths of 1 percent of it to provide all the heat and light on which all of life on Earth depends. Stars larger than Sol fuse not just hydrogen into helium, but helium into carbon, nitrogen, and oxygen.

As I looked at the Lagoon Nebula, knowing that the carbon of my flesh and the calcium of my bones were fused in stars formed in just such nebulae that lived and died before the sun was born, the kinship I had always felt for Earth expanded across the emptiness of interstellar space to embrace the stars. Arcing up from Sagittarius, the Milky Way, the disk of stars that is our home galaxy stretched above me in a shining blur of stars, nebulae, and dark clouds of dust where other infant stars may still be cocooned. In the eastern sky, the birds of summer rose in the summer triangle. This bright triangle rises in the evenings of early summer and lingers high in northern skies until slowly plunging toward the western horizon in midwinter. It's made up of the stars Deneb (the tail) in Cygnus the swan, Altair (the flyer) in Aquila the eagle, and Vega in Lyra the lyre, whose name means swooping eagle. On a truly dark night these starry birds can

---

10. Ten joules is the energy to lift one kilogram (2.2 pounds, roughly the weight of one liter of water) one meter.

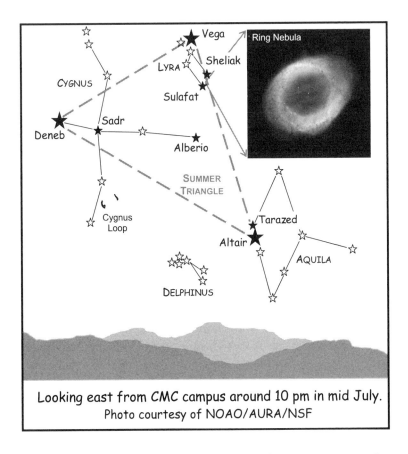

Looking east from CMC campus around 10 pm in mid July.
Photo courtesy of NOAO/AURA/NSF

seem to swoop so low that I can almost grasp them to soar across the Milky Way with them. But, like blood crusted on an eagle's talons, the remnants of stellar death lurk amid the beauty.

The bright stars in the constellation of Lyra make a stick figure of a small triangle attached to a little parallelogram. Vega is in the triangle and between the stars at the far end of the parallelogram lies the Ring Nebula. This round smudge, a favorite of amateur astronomers, is the remnant of a sun-sized star and shows the fate of the sun some 5 billion years from now when it will swell to engulf the inner planets and eventually blow off its outer layers to leave behind its core as a white dwarf.

Farther north along the Milky Way, off the eastern wing of Cygnus, is the twenty-five-hundred-light-year distant Veil Nebula. It forms part of the Cygnus Loop, the remnant of a star that exploded twenty thousand years ago. Giant stars, in an "onion" structure of layers, fuse helium atoms to create neon, magnesium, silicon, sulfur, nickel, and iron (other light elements are also produced, but in much smaller amounts). When the star fuses iron into anything heavier, it doesn't release energy, but absorbs it, cooling the innermost core, which contracts as all gases do when cooled.[11] Layers above this core suddenly find themselves unsupported and fall in, causing the star to collapse from the inside out. By the time other layers fall in toward the center, it has become so dense that they bounce, sending a shock wave outward that blows the star apart in a supernova. Since the original iron and nickel core is destroyed in the collapse, the supernova explosion is the only place the universe can successfully create iron and all the heavier elements on the periodic table.

Standing on the CMC campus, breathing the products of sun-sized stars so that the supernova-forged iron in my blood could carry oxygen to my brain, a desire to know not just the Earth, but the entire universe took hold in me. For all my frustration with physics, I had a faint inkling that it might be my future. In the student union, as I was clearing tables to lay out a buffet, I came across a poster from the New Mexico Institute of Mining and Technology. It had a stack of post cards one could send off for information. I checked the box for the Ph.D. in astrophysics and sent it off. It took another year before I could admit my dream enough to change my major to physics. I was never certain I could succeed, not having taken the standard high school path to a career in science, but under the stars I did think it just might be worth the risk. Eleven years later, Tech would actually award me that degree.

---

11. To experience this, blow up a balloon on a very cold day and take it outside. It will shrink as the air inside it cools. For another fun phenomenon in the cold, next time it's colder than –20 degrees F, go out with some bubble stuff and blow bubbles. Most will break as they freeze, but some will sink to the snow and slowly deflate, creating little "onion skin" shells of bubble stuff. This is best followed, of course, by a steaming bowl of onion soup!

Chapter 4

Into the Weirdness

I N THE FALL OF 1978, I went to Fort Lewis College in Durango, Colorado, to pursue a degree in geology. But as CMC led me to explanations of the world I could see, at Fort Lewis, I would discover explanations of a universe within and beyond the mountains and deserts as weird and wondrous as Alice's Wonderland.

At Fort Lewis, my geology classes crept closer to my high school experience than my excitement at CMC. In mineralogy and invertebrate paleontology, I felt burdened by lists of chemical formulas and fossil phyla to memorize. Meanwhile, in physics, I started getting my feet on the ground and managed to pass the introductory course. Having now taught this course for many years, I refer to it as "fire hose physics" because learning physics from the encyclopedic text and the intense pace required to cover the material students are expected to have seen (though not necessarily understood) is rather like drinking out of a fire hose. One can get completely soaked and remain quite thirsty. Even so, physics intrigued me and thrilled me with its mathematical elegance. Finding geology unsatisfying, I searched for a different major since I still wanted to be a college professor with the opportunity to change lives as Dave had changed mine. Natural history attracted me, so I took the required introductory biology course. I didn't find much to interest me. It wasn't the field botany I'd delighted in at CMC, neither was it the zoology of National Geographic specials. It was reading through the book and memorizing cycles and names. There was so much to memorize! That was part of my disillusionment with geology! We had a lab component to the course, but I can't recall any of the activities. I stopped attending the classes and showed up only for the labs and exams. Again, I did reasonably well. I think I got a "B," but I didn't find it interesting. Perhaps if I had gone on in the natural history major, I would have found the biology more interesting and less of an exercise in memorization. I recognize that biology is, indeed, very interesting, and I enjoy learning about it, but the courses were deathly for me.

Meanwhile, back in physics, I took the sophomore course, modern physics. Unlike the sophomore courses in geology, modern physics is completely new material barely mentioned in the introductory course. The topics include special relativity, atomic and nuclear physics, and quantum mechanics. It is just about every physics student's favorite course. It was in this course that my interest in physics deepened to a lifelong vocation.

It was a second awakening to the universe, much like I had experienced in earth science at CMC, only this was not about what I could see, but about the incredible wonders beyond the reach of our unaided senses.

The nature of light is at the root of quantum mechanics. It had long been debated whether light is a wave or a stream of particles. In 1801, Thomas Young had shown that when light is passed through two closely spaced narrow slits, it results in a series of light and dark spots. This demonstrates the wave nature of light since particles would result in two overlapping bright spots as shown on the next page.

However, Albert Einstein in the 1905 paper that would win him the Nobel Prize in 1921, showed that *light* could be treated as if it were a stream of *particles,* which he called "quanta." The phenomenon he was explaining was that of the photoelectric effect, that current can flow from certain materials when they are exposed to light. This is the phenomenon behind solar cells.

The puzzle about this phenomenon was that whether or not current flowed depended on the color, the wavelength of the light, not

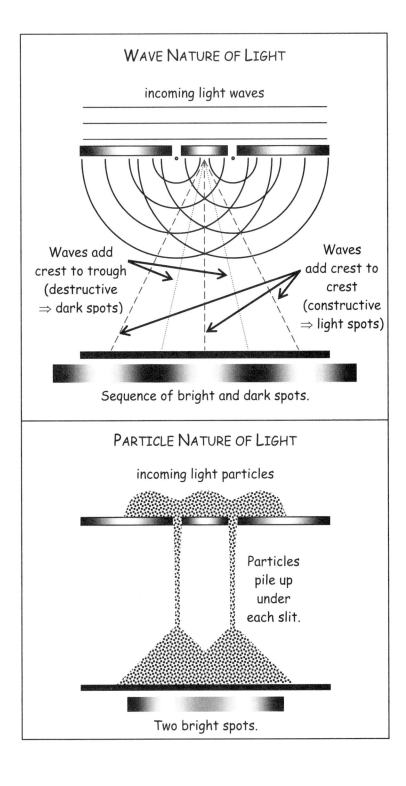

the intensity of the light. We can observe this with solar calculators that work in fluorescent light but not under some incandescent
lights or the low pressure sodium lights illuminating some parking
lots with their pale yellow glow. Once current was flowing, brighter
light could make more current flow, but if the wavelength was too
long, the light too red, increasing the brightness could not make current flow. In 1900, Max Planck had explained the radiation from an
opaque object (a blackbody) by postulating that light was composed
of tiny bundles of energy that he called quanta (hence "quantum"
mechanics) and are also known as photons. The energy of the photons is determined by the frequency of the light, $E = hf$, where f is
the frequency (in cycles per second, or Hertz), h is Planck's constant
with a value of 6.626×10^{-34} joule-seconds and E is energy in joules.
It takes 10 joules of energy to lift the weight of a liter of water, one
kilogram (2.2 pounds), one meter, so these are very tiny energies,
but very significant in the atomic world. Einstein postulated that for
the light to free electrons from their atoms in a metal, the energy
of the individual photons must be greater than the energy binding
the electron to the metal. The electrons could not collect photons
of lesser energy to build up enough energy to free themselves; they
needed a single photon of sufficient energy. Any energy above the
threshold needed was converted into the kinetic energy, essentially
the speed, of the electron.

This explanation required light to be streams of particles. Yet
Thomas Young's double slit experiment required light to be waves.
So what is it? Waves and particles are very dissimilar! Waves exist
across space and disappear if they stop. Particles exist in specific locations and transfer momentum and energy when they stop. We see
this quality of light in comet tails pushed away from the sun by its
photons. Waves don't generally do this,[12] as anyone knows who has
played in the ocean beyond the breakers. The incoming waves make
you rise and fall, but don't push you in toward the shore. The breakers

---

12. Electromagnetic waves acting on charged particles is one exception.

do push one around, but that's really a manifestation of the particle nature of water — back to the fire hose! If you have tried to move a floating object beyond your reach, a toy boat, say, by pushing the water at it, you know that the waves simply make it move up and down, they don't move it outward from the shore. Only splashing the boat will make it move outward. Waves can't push things. They're very different from particles. The idea that light is both a wave and a particle is completely incomprehensible! And yet, every experiment done to examine the nature of light has confirmed this idea. If an experiment requires light to be a particle, it exhibits particle qualities. If an experiment requires light to be a wave, it exhibits wave qualities. Light that has diffracted through a double slit, happily revealing the wave nature, can be shone on a detector that requires it to be a particle.

This is not the end of the weirdness. It turns out that matter also exhibits both wave and particle qualities. In 1924, Louis de Broglie theorized that electrons should also show wave-like qualities. This makes matter as weird as light as it allows for the phenomenon of quantum tunneling. Imagine an orange in a bowl on a counter. It has energy due to its position above the floor. If it's an egg and falls off the counter, that energy can be used to break the shell! Things in nature tend toward the lowest energy state, so if the orange has a path, a hole in the bowl and a sloped counter, it will fall to the floor. However, if the bowl is sound, the orange will stay within it, in spite of the close proximity of the lower energy state of the floor. For electrons, this is not the case. De Broglie determined the wavelength of a particle of matter to be $\lambda = h/mv$ where λ is the wavelength in meters, h is Planck's constant (6.63×10^{-34} joule-seconds), m is the mass of the particle (9.11×10^{-31} kg for an electron), and v is the speed of the electron. This wavelength is very tiny. A 150-pound person (about 70 kg) walking one meter per second (about 2 miles per hour — a leisurely pace), has a wavelength of $(6.63 \times 10^{-34})/(70 \times 1) = 9.4 \times 10^{-36}$ meters. Tiny. The wave nature of a walking person is ridiculously small and does not manifest itself in any meaningful way. But for electrons in metals like copper, their tiny masses make the wavelength significant and the wave qualities of electrons do manifest themselves in strange ways. One of the first uses of this was in electron microscopes. In these, electrons are used instead of light to "illuminate" materials under study. These are used because the wavelengths of the electrons are smaller than those of light, making electron waves capable of "seeing" much smaller structures than light. In today's electronic devices, the wave nature of matter is manifested in quantum tunneling. Back to the orange in the bowl on the counter: replace it with an electron[13] in an isolated bit of silicon in a computer chip. A sort of "electron bowl" that acts as a switch that is either "on" when an electron is there (giving it a value of 1 in binary code) or "off" when no electron[14] is present (a binary 0). The sides of the bowl are created by some insulating material, often a glass or ceramic, separating the bit of silicon from the wiring in the circuit where electrons can flow freely to do things like create these letters as I type. Unlike the orange, if the wiring is at a lower energy level (acting as the floor in the orange example), the electron has a finite probability of crawling out of its bowl to get to that lower energy level. I think of the wave nature of the electron in this case as being rather like spider's legs feeling around the bowl searching for a lower energy level. Once a lower energy level is found, the tip of that leg becomes the electron, itself, tunneling out of its bowl. The probability that any given electron will tunnel out of its bowl is tiny, not much larger than your chance of winning the lottery (given that you've bought a ticket!), but there are bazillions of electrons in any given bowl — to create one volt of electricity, spread 55,000 electrons on a plate 1 millimeter square and the same number of protons on another, then separate the plates by one millimeter.

---

13. Actually, bazillions of electrons, but the orange analogy works best if we limit ourselves to one.

14. Actually some minimal value of electrons so that their collective charge is effectively zero.

QUANTUM TUNNELING OF AN ELECTRON

Higher energy

An electron tunnels through an energy barrier such as silicon in a computer chip.

Lower energy

Lower energy

An electron on the left can only cross the high energy barrier if it is a wave. Particles simply bounce off the barrier.

QUANTUM TUNNELING ANALOGY FOR AN ORANGE

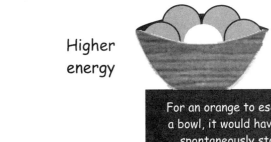

Higher energy

For an orange to escape a bowl, it would have to spontaneously stop existing in the bowl and begin existing at the lower energy level of the floor.

Lower energy

However weird this sounds, it is in use every day in our electronic devices. Anything that uses "flash" memory — "memory stick" USB flash drives, most cell phones, digital cameras, etc. — makes use of this effect. Electrons, matter, really are waves! Everything in the solid world, rocks, tables, my own skin, is, at the subatomic level, made of stuff that is both particles and waves. Looking at the world with this understanding, it soon becomes very hard to understand what "real" means.

This was the world of physics I was discovering as my geology classes devolved into memorization. When I changed to an advisor in physics, my geology advisor commented that he found it odd that my mathematics score on the college entrance exam (the ACT, more commonly used in the West at that time, not the SAT) had me in the fifty-sixth percentile, yet I was changing to a mathematical science. I realized that I didn't have the academic pedigree or background thought necessary to study physics and was not sure I'd succeed. In graduate school this plagued me with low confidence in spite of succeeding at every step, including earning a Ph.D. But feelings are often blind to evidence. To this day I don't feel smart enough to be a physicist. But that's ok. I'm an astronomer!

There was little astronomy for me at Fort Lewis, though I did pursue it in special topics courses and independent studies, including a senior thesis on the interstellar medium. It was at New Mexico Tech that my knowledge of the larger universe deepened and expanded.

Chapter 5

Interior Darkness Descending

I CAN STILL SEE the afternoon sun casting shadows of the cottonwood trees onto the sidewalk that I walked every day. It was a typically beautiful and warm spring day in 1971 as I walked home from South Junior High School. Crossing the street onto the block where we lived, I recall thinking of how content I was. I was nearly twelve, in the seventh grade, and thought that I would like to stay in the seventh grade forever because I was so happy. I suppose that scene got fixed in my mind because of how prophetic it would later seem.

The darkness didn't arise due to an event, though events certainly deepened it. It more seeped in, like the chill of winter seeping in through ill-fitting windows or the tendrils of vines working their way through cracks in concrete patios. Looking at where it appeared in my history, I can't help but believe that the depression diagnosed when I was thirty-seven began with the hormonal upheaval that was puberty. I don't recall the process, just that seemingly days after that happy seventh-grade girl walked up Peoria Street from school, a morose teenager woke up in her body.

There were certainly issues to be morose about in those days. I had turned 10 in the banner year of 1968. I recall my mother waking me up in June with the words "There was another shooting last night" as she told me of Robert Kennedy's death. My sisters were home from college so I was sleeping on the couch in the living room. The words took me back to Martin Luther King's death months earlier and President Kennedy's death in 1963. The first thing I recall watching on television was John Kennedy's funeral. John Junior was a little more than two years younger than I as we both watched the riderless horse following the flag-draped casket. Neither of us truly understood what was happening, but we both knew we were present at a profound moment for our nation and for his family. With that, followed two years later by Malcolm X's assassination, then King and another Kennedy, assassinations became a not unexpected part of our civil life. With the deaths of MLK and RFK, though I was still only a child, I began to sense a dimming of a hope in my country. They were killing the good ones. They were killing the ones who looked "at things as they are not and said, 'Why not?'" They were also killing our older brothers and a few of our sisters in Vietnam. We lost 16,589 in 1968 and would lose another 17,000 before I crossed the street in the spring of 1971 thinking of how happy I was.

There was hope that burned bright in those years. Astronauts of the *Apollo 11* and *Apollo 12* missions had walked on the moon in 1969, making us all look at the moon differently. It was a place. A place where we could stand looking back at Earth as the tiny garden in the darkness that it was. We still gathered around TVs to watch every *Saturn V* rocket launched from Cape Kennedy, named for the dead president we could all quote saying, "We will go to the moon in this decade not because it is easy, but because it is hard." We also watched every return, waiting breathlessly for the sighting of the parachutes carrying the capsule back to Earth.

But death lurked even among the shiny and powerful rockets. In 1967, astronauts Grissom, White, and Chaffee died in their training capsule on the ground. In the spring before my contented walk home from junior high, the astronauts of *Apollo 13* struggled to return to Earth without walking on the moon, having had to use the oxygen in the Lunar Lander to stay alive. Though we had recovered from that near tragedy well enough for *Apollo 14* to have successfully journeyed to the moon and returned in February of 1971 with the essential mission accomplished, support for it waned, and the last *Apollo* would splash down into the Pacific in December of 1972.

In spite of the events of those years, I'm not sure there was much that was unique about my depression. It seems that many teenagers — my nieces and nephews and children of my friends — go through morose periods. But mine didn't abate with the years and was deepened by personal experiences.

One of those events was the sexual assault I suffered at fourteen. It was a horrible event that left me frightened of just about everything for the next twenty years. Not only did I know that bad things *could* happen to me, I assumed they *would*. I realized that I had assumed that if I was good (I was reasonably good outside of being morose and smoking cigarettes) the Great White Father God I was told of in catechism class would protect me. God hadn't protected me that night and I felt betrayed by the universe. The night that I had previously found comforting, became malevolent. I had begun accepting my female body — after the failure of my childhood efforts to kiss my elbow (legend held that that would turn me into a boy). My body now became something I loathed. Every time I went to the bathroom, I was disgusted anew with the genitals he had touched, wishing there was some way to rid myself of them. It was as though I blamed my own body for the assault more than I blamed my assailant.

The greatest effect, though, was that death, my own random, meaningless death on an unremarkable Tuesday evening became real. I had met my mortality and would never again be free of that knowledge. The possible randomness and meaninglessness of my death seared my unexamined childish belief in God. We'd been taught that God had a plan for each of our lives, but if some guy could kill me on an ordinary night for no better reason than that I was female, what kind of plan was that?

My worldview was completely shaken. God was not reliable, the president seemed to be a crook, the war continued, and the *Apollo* program was over. There was no longer the will or the funds to send men to the moon as the legacy of Kennedy receded into a past quickly being idealized as a Camelot that existed outside reality. My trust for the universe and all those who had taught me of it disappeared into a nagging hunch that life was truly meaningless and God, if God existed, was not trustworthy. In those days we weren't rushed off for counseling or spiritual healing. Though I was given some time away from school and my parents and family were tenderly kind, I was expected to put the event behind me and get on with the ordinariness of life. And so I did as well as I could, though I was not always able to hide my profound fear of the world.

All was not bleak. There were things that buoyed my spirit and engaged me in life. The following August, my sister and her husband generously included me in a trip to Alaska, which deepened my love for nature with its vast and magnificently beautiful vistas. The following year, my parents took me with them to Ireland to meet cousins in County Kerry and an uncle in Dublin. With the Watergate scandal nearing its peak, the situation in Vietnam looking bleak, and bitter divisions over the war deepening, few of us kids, even from a military town, were proud of our country. When my parents took me to Ireland, I found more than connections, history, and beauty, I found an identity and for many years became very Irish.

Life went on. I graduated from high school and went to college. In my second year at CMC, my friends and I were planning a spring break road trip to San Francisco. Back in Aurora, our neighbor, and one of my better friends from high school, had lung cancer. Pearl was in her eighties and had been my one friend on the block during high school. It started by my shoveling the snow off her walk. I don't believe she paid me and, likely, it was my parents who told me it was a good thing to do for a neighbor. After one of the first times I shoveled, she invited me in for something to drink. To my surprise, it was a screwdriver! We sat and drank and chatted. We finished and she offered a second, which we savored for a long while. Two was her strict limit, and I can't say I was drunk, but I left her house with a warm buzz. We discovered a friendship over those drinks that sustained us both through my high school years. Our discussions spanned across decades from her growing up and raising a son in Ryan, Iowa, to my trials at school. She had taught school in Iowa for many years and moved to Colorado with her husband, James, late in life to be near her son and his family. James, a taciturn man, scared me as a child (for no good reason; he just looked scary), but I had always liked Pearl, who let me cut thorough her yard to play with my pals across her back fence.

Pearl's back yard butted up against the back yard of my pals on the block, Danny and David. Also, her granddaughter, Pat, would often stay with Pearl and was one of the very few girls in the local neighborhood. So Pearl was in my life most days. Danny and David had a large maple tree in their back yard and all us kids spent many a glorious day climbing among its branches. Pearl would often come out her back door to yell at us to come down, afraid of our falling. We complied until she went back into her house, and then scrambled up again. She complained to my mother about our climbing. My mother, after five other children, took the danger in stride, figuring it was better for us to be in a tree in the yard than off in the neighborhood seeking other types of entertainment.

By the time I was in high school, Danny and David, sons of an Air Force officer, had moved away, as had almost all my friends. I think it was as hard to be the only non-military brat in the neighborhood as it was to be the military brats who were always moving. Pat had her own life and friends in her parents' neighborhood and visited Pearl more rarely, so Pearl became my only friend in those years.

In the spring of 1978, my parents let me know that if I wanted to see her alive again I had better skip the road trip. Unbeknown to either of us, we had shared our last screwdriver the previous summer as she was too sick at my Christmas break to enjoy one. She was quite frustrated when I first showed up in the spring because she was too exhausted to even chat. I assured her it was all right, but she said, "No, dammit! I want to talk!" Pearl died in the middle of the week I was home. During the last afternoon I spent with her, I don't know if she knew I was there. She was lying on her back and would try to put her hands on the pillow above her head. I imagine it made breathing a bit easier. She could get her hands there, but didn't have the strength to keep them there so I held them for her. I spent a couple hours there beside her, holding her hands above her head. At one point I thought she may have squeezed my hand but I can't be sure. That night, I awoke with a start to a single peal of thunder and sensed that she was dead. Pearl was the first person close to me who died. It brought the reality of my own mortality back to haunt me through the last weeks of my time at CMC. I was most bothered by not knowing where Pearl was. I had known the person and seen the body in the casket with the person no longer there. All the Catholic rituals spoke of angels and heaven, but I no longer believed them. I didn't know what to believe about death and was forced to simply leave it as a question, a nagging unknowing that would arise at odd moments and leave me frightened of the universe.

At Fort Lewis College, I came to an answer on another winter night. My friend Debbie had been having problems with school and family. One glittering night with the temperature in the teens, she was coming to the end of her rope. She told me all the reasons that she did not want to go on living and, to my despair, I could not manage to counter any of them. In spite of my depression and creeping spiritual darkness that had me contemplating suicide myself fairly often, I still believed that it was better to stay alive than to die. I had been working with a counselor at the college and, knowing I was out of my depth with Debbie, I called her for help. She called her supervisor and the night ended with the police handcuffing Debbie and forcing her into a squad car as she screamed obscenities at me for having set things in motion. Later she did thank me for what I'd done, but walking back to my dorm room that night, I recall standing in the snow and looking up at the star-filled sky. The sky was beautiful. Shards of low clouds were turned to a warm pink by the campus lighting in stark contract to the deep black of the sky and glittering of the stars. I stood enthralled by the beauty, but feeling a deep emptiness. As I looked, I realized that all I saw there in the depths of the night were stars. There was no benevolent spirit beyond the roof of the sky. There was no God. There was just the enormous depth of the universe indifferent to this small creature of the Earth.

It was the most mystical experience I've ever had, that view of the sky. I hadn't realized that for all the shakiness of my belief in God, I couldn't quite conceive that God did not exist. God was too knitted into my Catholic experience, my assumptions, and even my language. That night I did conceive that God did not exist and saw a universe animated only by the processes of physics, chemistry, and biology, and it left me profoundly lonely. The cold seemed to sink into the depth of my bones and my soul where it lingered for months and can still arise at unexpected moments.

Looking back now as a person of faith, my sense of that night is that I let go of the floundering raft of my childhood belief and drifted out into the cosmic ocean where I would have to make my home.

Chapter 6

Into the Vastness

I WAS TERRIFIED of graduate school. When I chose a graduate school, I looked for a program I thought I could get out of (with a degree), not the best program I could get into. I was not at all confident I could succeed. At the New Mexico Institute of Mining and Technology (Tech), the fear of failure nearly sent me running in my first week. I was assigned to give a lecture on comet nuclei in our "astrophysical seminar," where one of the graduate students had to lecture on an assigned topic. This was always a source of intense work and high anxiety as the faculty always asked questions beyond our understanding. I knew nothing about comet nuclei and had only a few days to prepare a graduate-level talk, but was determined to go down with some style if I was going to flunk out in my first week. Fortunately, I had kissed the Blarney Stone when my parents took me to Ireland, and, indeed, it seemed to give me "the gift of gab." Ignorant as I was of comets when the topic was assigned, I managed to learn just enough to give a reasonably good talk, to the surprise of some of the faculty who were quite complimentary, in spite of the fact that I mostly used *Scientific American*, not the research literature (there's only so much one can learn in a few days and I had thought it better to understand what I was talking about at a slightly lower level than to blither uncomprehendingly at a higher level. It's a tactic I've stuck to and it seems to work rather well!).

That first talk on comets and the semester's worth of talks by myself and other graduate students got me interested enough in comets to seek a summer research position at the Joint Observatory for Cometary Research (JOCR, pronounced "joker") directed by a professor at Tech.

The observatory was on a ridge of South Baldy, the highest mountain of the Magdalena range, just west of Socorro. The peak has an altitude of 10,783 feet, but the observatory was on a saddle below it. From the observatory, we could see the lights of Socorro, six thousand feet below, the glow from Albuquerque, seventy miles north, and lights from a few isolated ranches. This made the sky darker than any I had known and gave me the opportunity to learn not just the bright stars, but fainter stars and nebulae that appear as faint smudges in a truly dark sky.

On a typical night in July, as darkness descended and we began our observations, Ursa Major, the Great Bear, partly made up by the Big Dipper, was descending to walk along the northern horizon through the night as Leo the Lion plunged below it. From the Dipper, following an "Arc to Arcturus" from its handle and continuing with a "Spike to Spica," encircled the constellation of Coma Berenices, named for the hair of Queen Berenice of Egypt. In 245 BCE, legend holds, she cut a lock of hair off as a sacrifice to the gods for the safe return of her husband (and brother), Ptolemy III, from the Third Syrian war. The lock disappeared from the altar where she left it and the astronomer, Conon, claimed it had been placed among the stars by the gods.[15] Lacking in bright stars, Coma seems empty in light-polluted skies, but from JOCR, the cluster of stars from which it derives its name glittered in the west, covering about 5 degrees, the width of my fist held at arm's length. Due north of us in the plane of the galaxy, the great "frisbee" of stars in which we live, it is on a galactic orbit nearly parallel to the sun's. The cluster is about 288 light years away, contains about 80 stars, and is estimated to be 400 to 500 million years old. Thus when life was in early stages of evolution, these stars were forming from gravity's action on an interstellar cloud.

---

15. Backyard Astro.com. Backyard Astronomy for Amateur Astronomers. See online *www.backyard-astro.com/focusonarchive/comaberenice/comaberenice.html.*

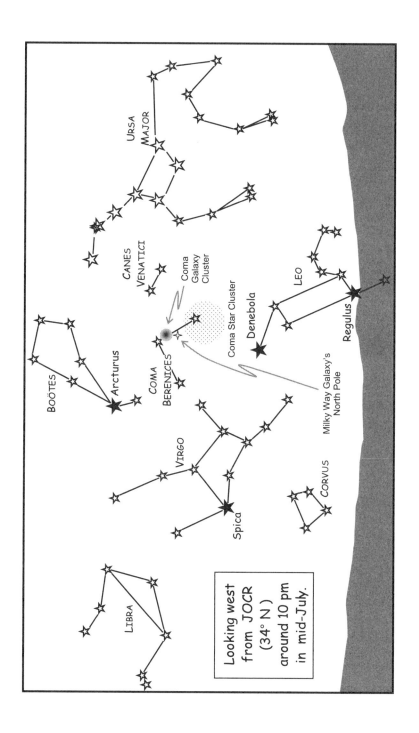

Looking west from JOCR (34° N) around 10 pm in mid-July.

To the south, the plane of the Milky Way arched up from the horizon through the brilliant constellations of Scorpius, marked by the bright red star, Antares, "rival of Ares (Mars)." This large constellation, and Sagittarius to the east, straddles the plane of the Milky Way in the direction of its center, 30,000 light years away. It is about this distant center that the sun and its attendant planets orbit every 250 million years. Between us and this center, the galaxy is thick with stars, bright nebulae, and thick clouds of opaque dust and gas in which the universe is creating new stars with its ancient recipe of gas and gravity. With my unaided eye, I could pick out numerous fuzzy blurs. Between the tail of the scorpion and the teapot asterism of Sagittarius is a bright star cluster described by Ptolemy the astronomer in 130 BCE. It is about 800 light years from us, a mere 2.5 percent of the way to the center of our galaxy. Another easily observed blur was the Lagoon Nebula where hydrogen gas, heated by newly formed stars, glows red against even more distant star fields. The Hubble Space Telescope has revealed "twisters" and "star wisps" in the darker, denser parts of the nebula[16] where yet more stars are forming from the cosmic recipe of hydrogen, gravity, and time.

The winter solstice is found near the Lagoon Nebula. We think of it as a date, but it is also a position in the sky along the path of the sun that is farthest south in our sky. On the summer solstice, this point is due south at midnight, then takes this position earlier and earlier until the winter solstice when it's there at noon.

The night's observing had begun before sunset as we loaded photographic plates into frames that we would lock into place at the prime focus of the telescope. The telescope, known as the comet camera, was not large since its purpose was to photograph wide fields covering the long comet tails extending away from the sun. The work of observing was to guide the telescope so that it followed the motion of the comet, slightly different from the motion imparted to the stars due to the rotation of the telescope's platform, the Earth. Though the

---

16. Hubble Site Images, *www.hubblesite.org/newscenter/newsdesk/archive/releases/1996/38/*.

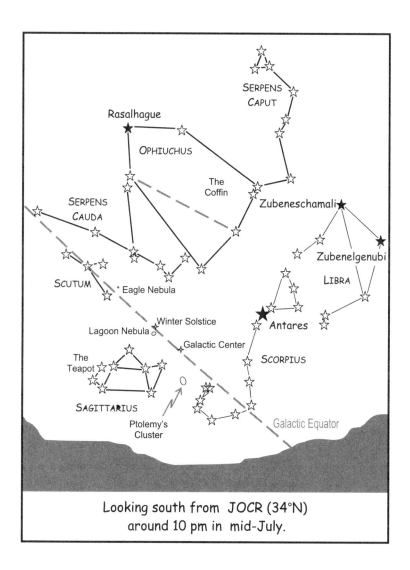

SERPENS
CAPUT

Rasalhague

OPHIUCHUS

The
Coffin

Zubeneschamali

SERPENS
CAUDA

Zubenelgenubi

LIBRA

SCUTUM

• Eagle Nebula

Winter Solstice

Antares

Lagoon Nebula

Galactic Center

SCORPIUS

The
Teapot

SAGITTARIUS

Ptolemy's
Cluster

Galactic Equator

Looking south from JOCR (34°N)
around 10 pm in mid-July.

motion of the comet was undetectable to us, seeming to be in nearly the same place night after night, it would blur the long-exposure photographs if we did not account for it. To accomplish this, we had a small guiding telescope with lighted cross-hairs attached to the main telescope. Knowing the comet's orbit from others' observations, we calculated the comet's motion with respect to a nearby star. We then set the telescope's coordinates on the comet and our guide scope on the star. At regular intervals, sometimes as short as five or ten seconds, we would move the telescope a calculated amount in the direction of the comet's motion. We did this by rotating a calibrated knob to move lighted cross hairs and then moving the telescope to put the guide star back at the center of the cross hairs. We would do this for stretches up to an hour with a few minutes between observations all night long. Though a generally exciting and delightful way to earn a paycheck, there were parts of this job that were truly work. First was that we observed during the dark of the moon, generally between third quarter and first quarter, so that the skies were dark. This prevented us from just changing over to the night shift since we were on the day shift in the lab during the bright of the moon. So staying up all night never lost its challenge. During the observations, timing was done by listening to WWV, the radio signal broadcast from Fort Collins, Colorado, that all our "radio controlled" clocks now use. We didn't have a clock; we had a little radio that tuned to 5, 10, or 15 MHz and listened to the broadcast ticks (or were they tocks?) of the time signal interspersed with announcements of the time "At the tone, six hours, forty-seven minutes, coordinated universal time. Bong. Bong. Bong...," some weather announcements, and warnings of solar electromagnetic storms that could affect radio communications. Counting the ticks between guiding adjustments without getting distracted by the announcements tended to get more difficult as the night progressed. A further complication of this arose from the fact that our guide scope was rigidly attached to the telescope that, of course, could point at any position in the sky. This meant that the eyepiece of the guide scope could be in just about any position. Rarely were we able to sit or stand comfortably to look through the eyepiece. More often it was in an awkward position that required us to stoop, stand on a stool leaning precariously, or take some other position that became more and more uncomfortable and difficult as the long exposure proceeded. It also got more difficult as the night went on and we got tired and cold.

We would often have up to ten minutes between exposures. Not wanting to ruin our night vision, we couldn't read, so we would chat, or, more often, simply stare out the dome at the sky. Between the bright stars of Scorpius and the Summer Triangle lies the large constellation of Ophiuchus (oh-fee-YOU-ks), the Snake Bearer. There are few bright stars in the constellation and though it represents Esculapius, the Greek god of healing whose patients never died, one particularly dark stretch of sky is recognized as the asterism of "The Coffin." Staring out at this darkness, a prickle on the back of my neck would remind me of that night at Fort Lewis and I would see again the indifferent darkness instead of the underside of heaven. The vast darkness was too much for me to see so I would turn away to take cover in the confines of the dome and refuge in the details of my work. For all my love and fascination for the sky, I wanted to hide from its vastness so as that I wouldn't have to confront my loss of comfort, my loss of God.

After two years of photographing comets, I left the mountain for the Very Large Array (VLA) Radio Telescope stretching across the Plains of San Augustin in New Mexico to study galaxies for my Ph.D.

Chapter 7

An Astronomer's Curiosity

FINDING MYSELF turning away from the night sky made me aware of how my sense of nature had changed. As a kid, I used to spend hours sitting in trees. Dangling above Peoria Street with its endless stream of cub scout–laden station wagons whose tires indelibly tracked and embossed the texture of the street on the spelling and arithmetic papers dropped and forgotten by those of us who never got gold stars for our efforts at the elementary school three blocks down, I never thought to be afraid of falling. There with the leaves and the bugs I was at ease with my universe; the tree was strong, the bugs didn't bite, and the blue ceiling of the sky capped everything and kept it safe. As I sprawled there, though, curiosity grew: Why are the leaves green? Why is the sky blue? What's above the sky? As climbing trees became more difficult with the years, the curiosity grew stronger, finally drawing me away to a study of science far from my comfortable perches. I've learned a lot in my studies. Science has taught me of wonders and details overlooked by more casual observers. Red rocks speak to me of warm, shallow seas that were never mapped or sailed. Trees bring to mind the yet unexplained explosion of familiar plant life 75 million years ago that coincided with the sudden and dramatic extinction of the great reptiles. And the sky is not a ceiling at all. The universe is a wonder-full place to live and an endless source of delight for a curious mind. I gained much in learning why the sky is blue and why the sun shines. But in the equations and the theories I lost something that I didn't even know I had when I was at home in the trees. As I studied the universe it has become curiously strange to me and I became foreign. The comfort that I once knew was lost.

In all learning, something is lost, a price paid in the forfeit of ignorance. When the first atomic bomb was detonated at Trinity site, New Mexico, in 1945, we grasped the power of the stars. That grasp is bought with our fear; not an adrenaline-filled fight or flight reaction to immediate danger, but an ever present sense of dread borne by the survivors and inheritors of the cold war. Our hope in tomorrow is fragile. Our confidence in the face of death that life will continue has become a shadow of what it was for previous generations. Life may end. The future may be lost.

The atomic bomb, though, was built to win the future. During the early years of its development it was the Allies' hope against the Nazis. The work of the scientists and their students was motivated not only by their love of science, but also by terrifying visions of jackboots run amuck. But VE Day preceded Trinity. It was Japan, not Germany, that reaped the bitter fruits of that awesome collection of minds that was the Manhattan Project. The bomb was dropped to save lives, so they said; the lives of the soldiers of both armies massed for the invasion of Japan. And so it did. Those soldiers saved became the fathers and professors of those of us who can appreciate but not fully comprehend the hope that they once vested in that most terrible of weapons; those of us whose nightmares were inspired by schoolroom exercises in "duck and cover" and constant reminders that the bombs could drop at any minute; those of us who have known only these years so insidiously and darkly shadowed by the threat of annihilation. It is not our fear that makes us unique among the generations, for there have always been famines and wars enough to fear. We are set apart instead by our awful hopelessness in the face of our own creation. The incredible destructive power of our weapons affords us no compromise. We know enough of their effects to be convinced that, burned and blinded, sifting through the ashes of their civilization, the survivors will envy the dead. Thus fearing both death and survival we listen in stunned disbelief to talk of limited nuclear war and live on the edge of terror like soldiers who know that the next battle will be their last. Those soldiers have one last hope; if the battle does not take place they just may survive. So may we all.

Symbolic of our faith in that survival, the Space Shuttle landed at Northrop Strip, New Mexico, in 1982. Separated from Trinity by thirty-seven years and fifty miles of desert, the space ship is the future so compromised at ground zero. That future is bright against the darkness of our dread. It is the clean newness of spaceports. It is the confidence and power of *Enterprise* bursting into warp drive. It is the calm serenity of Spock's coffin, jettisoned to the keening of a lone bagpipe's "Amazing Grace," gleaming black against the varied greens of a new jungle; at rest on a new world.[17] Beneath a new sky blued by water and a yellow sun, there is peace. The Space Shuttle, leaping from a Florida marsh, seeks that peace. From a once vast planet that nuclear arsenals and satellite photographs have shrunk to a tiny garden dangling in the void, we reach out to the cosmos.

Just as tall ships once disproved the flatness of the Earth, so spaceships belie the flatness of the sky. No longer the bespeckled underside of heaven, the sky has become a place. The moon is a place where the rising of a crescent Earth marks the month. Mars is a place where a rusted sky looms over canyons where only dust now flows. Jupiter is a place. Ganymede and Io, Saturn and Titan are all places, worlds that our robots explore and on which we may someday stand. The stars, too, will become places as our telescopes, lifted above the fog of our atmosphere, reveal planets orbiting distant suns. Perhaps we will find a small planet where deserts bake and rains rise in swirling white from blue oceans. But whatever worlds we find beyond our solar system, our reach to them is frustrated by distances so great that we measure them in units of time. Light, traveling at 186,000

---

17. These images are from *Star Trek: The Motion Picture* released by Paramount Pictures in 1979.

miles per second, has taken four years to reach us from Alpha Cen-
tauri, the star closest to our sun. From the bright blue giant Sirius,
the light has been traveling for almost nine years. Thus as we stare
at the stars we see back in time. Look to Aldebaran in Taurus and
Enrico Fermi oversees the first sustained nuclear reaction under the
west stands of the first Stagg Field at the University of Chicago and
the scientists of the Manhattan Project work toward the first atomic
bomb that will build a mushroom cloud over an American desert.[18]
Look to Sadr, the belly of Cygnus the swan, and Columbus returns to
Spain from his discovery of the New World.[19] Look past our galaxy
to the galaxy in Andromeda and *Homo habilis,* the first species in the
genus *Homo,* hunts with flaked-stone spear points. Beyond this we
cannot see without telescopes for even the combined fires of a billion
suns cannot dispel the darkness of a thousand million light years of
intergalactic space.

For all that exists in the universe, it is mostly empty. The galaxies,
those swirling masses of dark clouds and bright stars, are mere sparks
in a sea of darkness. Shining red and blue, the nebulae where stars
are born are but brief flashes of color. Giant stars dying violently
in supernova explosions glow brighter than entire galaxies only to
become black holes that even light cannot escape. Our own sun, a
small yellow star shining its heat and light against the eternal cosmic
night, as well shall die. As it approaches its death it will expand;
its outer surface will cool from yellow to red and engulf the inner
planets. Then Earth and its trees shall be no more.

Mother Earth, who fostered so many species in salted oceans,
canopied jungles, and ageless grasslands is as mortal as the creatures
that have passed from her lands and seas into extinction. She and all
that remains with her will be vaporized as the expanding atmosphere
of the sun approaches. All that we know; the mountains, the flowers,
the fish, and the cities, will be reduced to the basic elements of which

---

18. Aldebaran is 65 light years away so as I write this in 2007 the light arriving from it
left in 1942.

19. Sadr is 522 light years away.

they are made and be blown back to the empty reaches between the stars. There is a comforting completeness in knowing that our physical substance, forged in the cores of stars, shall become again part of the interstellar dust from which new stars will be made. But we are more than our physical substance, or so we've always thought. Deep within the biochemical labyrinth of the human brain is a soul that contemplates and seeks a reason for its own existence. From the loneliness bought with our concept of self and the fear gained by our knowledge of death arises a need for meaning. In the pattern and structure of the universe and of us, we have sought purpose in our being. With powerful microscopes we have looked into the nuclei of our cells and studied our substance. Yet we are baffled by what we are. Digging sometimes with teaspoons, we have unearthed the track by which we evolved out of primordial oceans. But we still cannot determine how we came to have the minds capable of conceiving the questions that we ask. In the spectroscopic images of far-off nebulae we have discovered evidence of the organic compounds on which our entire biology is built. But in this vast universe extending past even our imagination's reach, we are yet alone.

Perhaps it is just that our young sciences need more time, more data before they can answer our deepest questions. Or perhaps the answers truly do lie in the theologies begun before we knew of black holes and DNA. But with the explosion of scientific discoveries and technological advances that has occurred since World War II, religion has become intellectually unfashionable. The concept of God has become absurd as we have discovered our own ability to create and to destroy. The habits and traditions of devotion have come to be seen as the foolish eccentricities of the old and the ignorant. By our academic conditioning, we who have inherited this Earth that the whim of governments can utterly destroy and who know too well our smallness as we stand at the brink of infinite space, have been denied that simple comfort of faith in ultimate goodness and reason that our grandparents, immigrating from famine-swept and war-torn lands, carried with their prayer beads and holy books carefully wrapped and bound with string.

As a graduate student, perched in an observatory more than a mile above the desert where Trinity and the space shuttle landing have faded into memories, I was no longer at ease with my universe. I was still delighted by it, awed by it, and absolutely fascinated by it. But I was also frightened by it. I had learned my astronomy well enough to know in the deepest core of myself that I truly stood upon a sphere surrounded by boundless space. My fear arose from my sense of insignificance and my terrible aloneness. Thus cursed with a curiosity too big and a courage too small, my mind reached out across the dark, cold infinity of spacetime to galaxies and quasars leaving me, a creature of warmth, light, and one small oblate spheroid, cowering, like a soldier in a foxhole with my face pressed to Mother Earth, straining to pull myself inside the womb of the blue planet that nurtured my species, so that I should never again look up to a moonless sky and glimpse the infinity beyond the stars. But the curiosity won and my face turned skyward. As I stared at galaxies as they were a million years ago, my soul, the legacy of my species, cried out to the night, out to the lights that so demanded my pondering. "Hello? Is there anybody else here?" But my cries were lost in magnetic storms and filter back to me as static on the AM band that I listened to when the fear had stolen my sleep. I wondered if I should ever again know the comfort that I once knew in the arms of trees. Or was this aching loneliness the price of my degrees? I searched within myself for a foundation on which I could build a faith that would console me. Though I found shreds of belief rooted in a child's awe of candles and incense, it was hope that had to be my base. I did not always believe in a God, but I did sincerely hope in one. By the dark of the moon, as I stood in the open dome of the observatory, an astronomer afraid of the sky, my prayer was that there was, indeed, someone to hear it.

Chapter 8

Choosing Faith

O N A RANDOM EVENING in the spring of 1982, as my first year
of graduate school was appearing to come to a successful end,
a small gray dog walked into my dorm room. Baca Hall was a two-
story stucco with each room opening to the outside. I lived at the
north end of the second floor and, as most of us did most of the time,
had my door standing open. I don't recall what I was doing when the
dog walked in and seemed to make herself at home. She was wearing a collar with a rabies tag and was quite sweet and affectionate,
apparently someone's pet who had gotten lost — or gotten dumped
as pets far too often are in that part of New Mexico. I got a friend
to drive me to the store for some dog food in case she was hungry
and accepted her as a guest for the night. In the morning, I called
Albuquerque to find the people behind her rabies tag. The tag had
been issued to an apricot poodle — a far cry from the gray furball
wearing it! The rabies registry gave me a phone number, which I
called to find that it was no longer in service. I didn't know what to
do. I hoped her people had moved to Socorro and, left on her own,
she would find her way home. She had a different idea. She followed
me across campus, patiently waiting outside the door when I went in
to check my mail. She then followed me to Weir Hall, which housed
the astronomy group. There were often dogs lounging around the
doorway, and I figured she would settle in with them until she went
on her way, hopefully back to her people. Instead, sitting in my office
I kept hearing the jingle of her single tag as she continually circled
the building looking for a way in. She managed it, and before long,

she appeared in the doorway of the office I shared with other graduate students, found me, and settled in under my desk. Apparently she was certain that I was her human, though it took me a few days to figure out that she was my dog. My office mates cared for her while I went to class and let me know that she was quite distressed to be left. So she was my responsibility. But I lived in a dormitory! I couldn't keep a pet. And, besides, though we'd had dogs at home, they hadn't been my responsibility, and I wasn't sure I was up for it. I was barely handling graduate school, how could I handle it *and* take care of a pet?

Well, the dog had already chosen me, so all I could do was figure out how to become her person. One of the professors agreed to take her in until the semester ended and I could get a apartment off-campus where I could make her a home. The professor's family named her "Lady," but I named her Queerbungle from a song on a Clancy Brothers album.[20] Most of the time, though, I called her QB, Qubers (with "Qub" pronounced as "cube"), which became Quberita with the Spanish diminutive, Furball, or, in her later years, Sweet Pea. We would be together for sixteen years during which she would teach me about unconditional love and save my life in bouts of deep depression. I will never stop missing her.

My journey to faith begins with QB because her arrival in my life was unexpected, inconvenient, and profoundly important. I was definitely her person. For whatever reason, I was the one she wanted to be with and she was not content with anyone else. At a time when my self-esteem and confidence sagged daily under the weight of graduate school, I was the most important person in the world to this little dog. When I arrived home, she would stand on her back legs pawing at me then turn in circles in a seeming dance of joy. Nothing buoyed my spirit as QB's attention and affection did. She followed me to every room, delighting my family by lying outside the

---

20. The song was "Bungle Rye" available on *The Best of the Clancy Brothers & Tommy Makem*, Legacy Records, 1994

bathroom door every time I went in. In her last years, even though she was deaf and blind, it would take her no more than ten minutes to migrate from one room to another, even though she was asleep when I left the first room. As an atheist I would simply say it was coincidence, but as I chose the path of faith, I saw QB as a timely gift from God inviting me back into trusting the universe at a time when I was open to that invitation.

I didn't dwell on ideas about God; it was simply a question present in the back of my mind. It dwelt there with the existential loneliness I'd felt since the night at Fort Lewis when I looked up to the sky to see only stars. As one on the path to becoming a professional scientist, since I could cite no objective data supporting the existence of God, I could not impose God on the universe. Thus I was an atheist; I could not bring myself to believe that God existed. And yet I had a longing for the sense of relationship with nature that I had had as a child sprawled in the trees. I still felt that sense at odd moments: on the first warm night of spring when the night sounds began again and rain scented the air so sweetly that I couldn't breathe enough of it. I denied it as anything real, considering it as a character flaw, a weakness, the imprinting of a Catholic childhood, or brain damage from early childhood exposure to incense. But it never went away.

Still feeling very Irish — hard to avoid with my name — I had come across *That Most Distressful Nation* by Andrew Greeley.[21] I found the book interesting and was intrigued by the chapter on the church, whose third sentence states "The Irishman clung to his religion as though it were all he had, and frequently it was."[22] Greeley explored the history of Irish Catholicism in Ireland and in the New World, not shying away from deep problems within the church and tensions between the Irish and Roman churches. I found it interesting as some explanation of the church my father, whose younger brother was a priest and younger sister had been a nun, had experienced, but

---

21. Andrew M. Greeley, *That Most Distressful Nation: The Taming of the American Irish* (Chicago: Quadrangle Books, 1972).
22. Ibid., 203.

did not feel any desire to return to any practice of Catholicism. That would come from another book by Greeley.

When I found out that Andrew Greeley was a Catholic priest, I was puzzled and amazed. Here was a man whose scholarly book I had enjoyed and he was a priest! I'd had little personal interaction with priests and had never found any of them engaging. My uncle was a priest but he had come to Colorado only once, when I was four. Priests seemed to be parts of that great mass of grown-ups that were basically uninteresting and certainly uninterested in me. The idea that one was a scholar and had written an interesting book completely lacking in religious platitudes was a startling idea to me.

When I came across Greeley's novel *The Cardinal Sins*, I was intrigued to read it.[23] Though many, particularly at that time, condemned his book as being too racy, I found it fascinating. He had characters, even priests, a cardinal, and women who were active Catholics and were thoughtful, interesting people. They didn't seem to agree with everything the church preached, and yet they stayed active in it. What a revelation it was that one could be involved in the church while maintaining intellectual integrity!

In the meantime, as I continued my intellectual journey into the weirdness and the vastness of the universe, it began to dawn on me how little our still young sciences really know of it.[24] The universe is always weirder than we expect. When equations hinted at the existence of black holes or the expansion of the universe, initial reactions were that these things were impossible. And yet we have since come to accept them as facts. At a more personal level, I count among the weirdnesses the facts that I exist and that I realize and ponder the fact that I exist. I seem to be more than my physical substance. My needs and desires seem to transcend survival and reproduction. If

---

23. Andrew Greeley, *The Cardinal Sins* (New York: Warner Books, 1982).

24. One of the jokes about the academic journey is that when you think you know everything, they'll give you a bachelor's degree. When you realize you don't know anything, they'll give you a master's. And when you realize that nobody else knows anything, either, they'll give you a Ph.D. Thus the realization of how little we know about the universe was exactly what I was supposed to be figuring out to qualify for my degree!

the universe is weird enough for me to exist, perhaps it is just weird enough for the whoness I sensed to be real. Perhaps the universe is just weird enough for God to exist — but it's going to be a far weirder God than they told me about in church!

Around the same time, I picked up a book by the author of the introductory astronomy textbook I had used at Colorado Mountain College. In *God and the Astronomers*, Robert Jastrow reviews the development of cosmology, the study of the origin and evolution of the universe.[25] In the early twentieth century, Edwin Hubble's observational study of galaxies revealed that all galaxies are moving away from us,[26] and the more distant galaxies are moving away faster. These are the raw data leading to the Big Bang theory of the origin of the universe. At first glance, these data could indicate that we're at the center of the universe and all the other galaxies are fleeing away from us. However, that explanation does not easily account for the fact that the more distant galaxies are moving away faster. The simpler explanation for these two data is that the space between the galaxies is expanding. In my classes I explain this as "Queerbungle Cosmology" with various QBs standing on a line that doubles in length, carrying the QBs with it as it expands. From any QB's point of view, the other QBs all move away, doubling their distance in whatever time the expansion takes place. The more distant QBs, to double their distance, have to move a greater distance than nearby QBs. Since the expansion for all the QBs takes place in the same amount of time, the more distant QBs must move faster than the nearby QBs. As Hubble was making his observations, Albert Einstein was developing his general theory of relativity. The mathematical formulation showed that the universe should be expanding. If it weren't expanding, all the matter would start rushing together due to the pull of gravity. Einstein, like all the scientists of his time,

---

25. Robert Jastrow, *God and the Astronomers* (New York: W. W. Norton, 1978).

26. Well, almost all. There are a few local galaxies moving toward us, such as the beautiful spiral galaxy in Andromeda, but this motion is due to the fact that we are gravitationally bound to those local galaxies so our motion does not reflect that of all the other galaxies we observe.

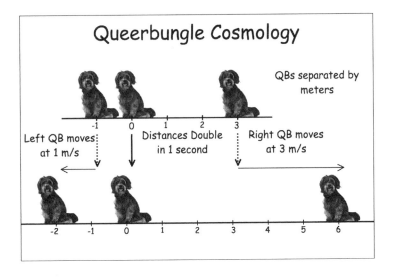

could not imagine an expanding universe, so he inserted a "cosmological constant" into his equations to force the universe to be static. He later referred to this as the "greatest blunder" of his life, though now it is seen as a prophetic anticipation of recently discovered "dark energy" that is accelerating the expansion of the universe. In 1927, a Catholic priest and physicist, Georges-Henri Lemaitre, published the expanding universe explanation of Hubble's data. It was derisively referred to as the "Big Bang" theory (with all the impolite connotations intended) by its critics, but has now come to be accepted as the best explanation of the data. Though we easily toss about the Big Bang theory today, the astronomers of the twentieth century were profoundly disturbed by the implication that it made the universe finite in time. Since the equations describing the expansion could be "run backward" in time, it forced us to accept that 13.6 billion years ago, the entire universe came into existence. The universe had a beginning. It was a jarring realization for the astronomers and physicists of the day and some prominent scholars refused to accept it, spending their lives seeking some other explanation of Hubble's pesky data and Einstein's pesky equations. The primary reason for their revulsion was that it made cosmology "too religious" in that it revealed a point in time when the universe could have been created by God. The great fear was that the religions would use the Big Bang theory to try to prove the existence of God. It never crossed their minds that, in fact, many religions would reject the theory because it didn't match their scripture timelines.

Robert Jastrow reflected on this startling evidence that the universe had a beginning and compared scientific cosmology to the creation story of the Bible, concluding that the Bible may be correct after all, stating:

> For the scientist who has lived by faith in the power of his reason, the story ends like a bad dream. He has scaled the mountains of ignorance; he is about to conquer the highest peak; as he pulls himself over the final rock, he is greeted by a small band of theologians, who have been sitting there for centuries.[27]

Though I did not buy that ending, the fact that an accomplished astronomer, one who claimed to be an agnostic, was writing of the possibility that there is some truth in religion freed me from the belief that scientific integrity forbade any consideration of the existence of God.

I read further, and puzzled about whether or not God could exist, looking for a compelling intellectual argument one way or the other. In this search, I realized that the authors of the books and articles on both sides were smarter, better informed, and more skilled at thinking through their arguments than I was. Yet these bright, well-read, articulate people came down on both sides of the question of God's existence. All the great philosophers have argued about this question and none have been able to remove all doubt from either conclusion. If they could, one argument or the other should

---

27. Jastrow, *God and the Astronomers,* 116.

be winning out and agreed upon by all scholars. But there are great scholars to this day that come to opposite conclusions.

Realizing this convinced me that the existence of God cannot be objectively determined. This meant that I had the freedom to interpret my own experience of the universe and come to my own conclusions about God.

The experience was threefold. Most prominent was the sense of who-ness in nature and the universe that, though I had tried to deny it as an atheist, never completely left me. On another side was the deep existential loneliness I had felt since the night at Fort Lewis when I looked up at the sky to see only stars extending into the vast depths of the universe. Looking back now, though it felt at the time that God was absent that night, what was truly absent was my childish view of God hovering above the ceiling of the sky. It was the faith equivalent of letting go of the side of the pool with its frightening sense of being on one's own. Lastly, there was the dark and profound fear of the world that had haunted me since the night of my sexual assault. I knew that if I wanted to make a positive contribution to the world, I needed a way to cope with the loneliness and fear. A way I could do that was to interpret my experience of the who-ness as a touch of God.

But what and who is this God? It certainly isn't the Great White Father of my Catholic childhood! That God didn't keep me safe from the guy with the shotgun. Any reading of a newspaper indicated this God didn't seem to be in the business of keeping anyone safe. And yet, in those moments when I was in touch with the who-ness, I did feel safe — and I felt loved.

So perhaps I was just fooling myself. Perhaps my sense of God was nothing more than a meditation state, a bio-feedback state of relaxation that flooded my brain with dopamine or some other calming chemical. Perhaps my seeking a way, an excuse even, to justify belief in God was a seeking of the "opiate" of faith to protect me from the reality of life and an indifferent universe. It very well may be. I have no objective evidence that my faith is not merely a coping mechanism to keep me from falling into nihilistic despair. Except that it *feels* real.

As a graduate student, I was being trained to revere data. Certainly, one is not to make up or fudge data. One is also not to disregard data, at least not without serious justification. In the end, my experiences of the who-ness and my sense of a relationship with a loving intelligence are data that honesty demands I not lightly disregard. Since these are internal, subjective, uncalibrated data, they can't be accepted uncritically, but neither can they be uncritically dismissed. My choice to believe in God was a choice to accept the data of my experience as being what they felt like. But, like any raw data, they needed to be calibrated and refined.

But how does one calibrate, refine, and derive information from the data of these ineffable, transient, purely subjective experiences? In science, calibrating one's instrument is usually reasonably straightforward and it's easy to compare measurements from different volt meters or different telescopes. Calibrating and comparing spiritual experiences is much more difficult. We can't know any spiritual or religious thing with the certainty that we can know the positions of stars or even the small margins within which we know the brightness of stars or the masses of planets. But the honest search for truth demands that we do all we can to compare our experiences with those of others also seeking truth and strive to discern what may hint at truth and what simply echoes our own desires and ego. This requires distancing ourselves from the experiences enough to be somewhat objective about them. And it requires the humility that all honest evaluation does: the realization that we may well be completely wrong and all our ethereal experiences may be nothing more than coping strategies of our own imagination and ego.

To begin learning about other people's experiences of God, I continued to read books and articles, but I also needed community. I needed others with whom I could discuss and explore what I was choosing to interpret as spiritual reality. As a start, I thought, perhaps I should reexamine the religion of my childhood. I didn't have to stay, but maybe it would help me on the journey (or not — I wasn't confident, but thought it worth the try). So much to my surprise, I made my way to Mass at the adobe church of San Miguel.

As do most Catholics after a long period away from the church, I felt I needed to go to confession before I could participate fully in Mass. I also wanted to talk to someone "religious" about this very odd and not very comfortable thing of wanting to believe in God and be part of a believing community. I still have the notes I made for that meeting listing my reasons for wanting to become a part of the church:

1. Depression and loneliness — needing something beyond myself

2. Needing the church to help me keep faith in the good times

   - it's easy to pray when in a heap
   - I need to maintain humility when I'm feeling strong

3. Want authority — sometimes I want someone to lean on

4. Want something constant in life

5. Curiosity — what do my parents, aunts and uncles and other Catholics find in the church?

6. Just feel impelled to seek it.

The priest, Fr. José, who would become a dear friend, gently listened to me and accepted me, giving me a warm hug of welcome as I left our meeting.

Once I went back to Mass, I couldn't get enough. I would go to every Mass on Sunday morning, including the 8:00 a.m. Mass in Spanish, even though my mastery of that language was limited to ordering at Mexican restaurants. I was intellectually hungry as well as hungering for the rituals. I continued to read about faith and spirituality, feeling no particular compunction to limit myself to

Christianity, let alone Catholicism. I read Thomas Merton's *Seven Storey Mountain,* and I read Thich Nhat Hanh's *Being Peace.* Since my leap of faith was to believe that this spirituality thing was real and valuable, the differences between the spiritual traditions seemed mostly about culture and history, not the spiritual truths all claimed to seek. When Bible studies classes were offered, I took them. If I had been at a major university with a religious studies department, I would have taken theology courses to slake my intellectual thirst for knowledge, but I was at a small technical university in a small, New Mexico town. It would be over a decade before I had a chance to slake some of that thirst with the Formation for Ministry classes offered by the Diocese of Ogdensburg in northern New York. At San Miguel, it turned out my journey was not intellectual; it was a journey of learning to be part of a community and friendship.

There were still religious sisters living in a convent at San Miguel. They were from various communities and mostly taught in the parish school that most of the children of the university and observatory staffs attended. Having always enjoyed singing, I got involved with the folk[28] choir and to know Sister Rosie, who played guitar for the group. She knew I lived alone and worked ridiculous hours so she'd often invite me to supper with her and Sister Carol. Fr. José, the pastor, was also there quite often. The first time they offered me a beer, it blew my mind. We shared many a meal and many a beer at the convent table and I came to know these people as the intelligent, thoughtful, and devoted individuals they are. Though we didn't have deep spiritual discussions, they taught me much about faith and seeking God by their generosity, tolerance, and willingness to spend their lives giving to others without expecting or receiving much in return. Their steadfast devotion to God, Christ, and the church coupled with their genuine generosity and interest in me helped me to see the church as a much more open and diverse community than

---

28. To this day, choirs that have guitars as their primary instruments are referred to as "folk choirs" to distinguish them from the traditional organ-led choirs.

its leaders would have us believe. I have met many genuinely good, thoughtful, and open people in the church, and I believe its members include many more such people than it does of the twisted predators and bumbling administrators who are more often in the headlines.

I took much comfort from the warmth of San Miguel parish and my friendships with Rosie, Carol, and José, but the decision that I could believe in God without being a fraud as an astronomer was fairly shaky. Since I had come to the study of physics much later than my peers, all of whom had excelled in math and science throughout their school years, I was terribly unconfident as a graduate student. Looking back, I don't know how I got through it with such minimal faith in my abilities. I think it might have been simply that I didn't know what else to do and it was easier to stay in school than to actually figure that out. With a constant feeling that I wasn't really smart enough to get a Ph.D., finding myself taking up religion in the midst of it left me feeling even more fraudulent as an aspiring astronomer. Some of the observatory staff were Catholics so it was not unknown at the observatory that I was Catholic. But I never expected to see any of the astronomers at Mass.

At the Saturday evening Mass, where the folk choir led the music, one of the choir members would lead the chanted responsorial psalm and also the Gospel acclamation: the Alleluia. One evening when I stepped up to begin the solo chant, I looked out into the congregation and completely lost my concentration as a few pews back sat one of the VLA's[29] senior astronomers. I managed to get through the chant without a meltdown, but remained stunned to see an astronomer, a real, accomplished astronomer there, at Mass. And he went to Communion! Years later when an astronomer from the Vatican Observatory showed up as the celebrant at the University of Arizona Newman[30] Center's noon Mass, the final death of my sense of

---

29. Very Large Array Radio Telescope, the instrument I used for my Ph.D. research.

30. University parishes in the United States are often referred to as Newman centers (e.g., St. Francis Newman Parish) because of Cardinal John Henry Newman, an Oxford Fellow and Anglican vicar who converted to Catholicism in 1845. Among his

fraudulence as a Catholic astronomer would nearly bring me to tears. The sense of fraudulence as a *feminist* Catholic astronomer remains — waiting to be put to death by a female astronomer celebrating Mass!

The astronomer who appeared at Mass was Bob Hjellming (JELL-ming, ignore the H) and that night began a long and deep friendship between us that lasted until his tragically early death from a heart attack in 2000. Bob was one of the aces. All his degrees were from the University of Chicago, where he had studied under the very best minds in astrophysics. As to why he had suddenly appeared at Mass, Bob admitted that after having been a part of the progressive Newman Center at Chicago where he had become a third order Dominican,[31] he had found the simpler, more rural, more conservative, less heady parish life at San Miguel oppressive and gave up on it. He did continue with a disciplined prayer life, and during the week before he appeared at Mass he said that in his prayer it had become clear to him that he had to rejoin the parish to mentor students from New Mexico Tech trying to maintain faith through the challenge of science or engineering studies contrasted with a rural Spanish parish. A Newman Association had been nurtured into existence by Sister Rosie and Jimmie, an English professor from Tech. Though it softened my sense of fraudulence to know Jimmie, it didn't cure it. When he left Socorro, leadership of the Newman group fell to Bob, Rosie, and me. We had meetings, often with meals, for the students, where we discussed prayer and the integration of faith and science. We didn't do anything remarkable with the group but did provide a venue for students to meet other Catholic Techies. Bob was quite a resource, having done serious study of the faith at Chicago. I did a lot of reading and much of the cooking that allowed us to offer the students non-cafeteria meals.

---

writings is *The Idea of the University,* where he says the aim of a university is the "enlargement of mind which is the power of viewing many things at once as one whole" (*www.newmanreader.org/works/idea/discourse6.html*).

31. Many religious orders and communities have a "third order" through which lay people become formal members of the community, though without religious vows.

The friendship between myself and Bob deepened on hour-long drives to or from the VLA site. We would get in the car and start chatting about some random topic and, more often than not, disagree about something. Being stuck in the car together for an hour, though, forced us to work through the disagreement to where we did agree. Neither of us ever changed our minds on the initial disagreement, but we did come to understand each other's reasoning.

Without Bob, I'm not sure I could have withstood the sense of fraudulence enough to continue with Catholicism. But since he was of an older generation with more trust in authority, our friendship didn't free me from it. That wouldn't come for decades.

Chapter 9

A View of San Miguel

AFTER MIDNIGHT MASS I could not bear to let the luminarias burn in the dark alone. So I took a little stool and, wrapped in my northern-New-York-winter parka, sat with my back against the adobe wall across the street from San Miguel Church and watched the flickering lights of Christmas set out to welcome the pilgrims who sought an inn so long ago. The temperature dropped toward zero as the stars of Orion dipped toward the west and hung glittering in the December night, over the flame-lit facade of the adobe church. The warm image of the adobe contrasted with the sharp cold of the winter night. The warmth I saw there, though, came from much deeper than the candle-lit brown exterior. The warmth I saw came from the years of knowing that church, both the building and the people who would be there to welcome the pilgrims of Christmas even if the building fell back to the dust and straw of which it is made.

I did not come to the church easily, but struggling through graduate school at New Mexico Tech found in myself a profound need to seek that presence, that thing greater than myself that I had always sensed, but had disregarded in college as a shred of immaturity, a lingering piece of a child's wish for an ordered, sensible, controlled universe with an eternal, benevolent parent controlling it. I had come to Socorro to study astrophysics, to immerse myself in a world of reason where the extraordinary phenomena of stars, galaxies, and the origin of the universe itself are explained with elegant, simple theories. To find in myself this persistent longing, this persistent need to seek this thing that did not fit into my physicist's universe was disturbing. Since I had other problems, a nagging lack of confidence and a fondness for alcohol, I was suspicious that my longing was, indeed, just childishness. But I was compelled to follow where it led, nonetheless. So I came to San Miguel. It saved my career and probably, my life.

As soon as I walked into that adobe church (with a Catholic friend because I was afraid to go alone after having been away for eight years), I knew I had come to a good place. People didn't jump up to greet me and welcome me back to the church with hugs and kisses the first time I walked into San Miguel; they simply made room for me in the pew and did not, in any way, question my presence there. Fr. José said that first Mass of mine. In his gentle homily and in the many that I heard in the years I was there, he let me know that I stood among those who came as I came, out of need. We came out of need for solace, for guidance, for hope, and for the companionship of others on the confusing, sometimes joyful, sometimes tragic path of life. As a child I had seen people at church as people who "knew the truth" and were simply going through the right motions to get to heaven. There may be some who do go to church for those reasons, but at San Miguel I learned of completely different reasons for going to church.

As I was welcomed into that community and became a part of it, I learned that most people go to church seeking some contact with God, but seeking even more to become better people here and now. Most people of San Miguel are there seeking to imitate Christ, and in that, seeking help in facing the realities of themselves, their relationships, and their lives. By the very act of choosing to attend Mass at San Miguel, a person admits a need, even if that need is just to keep the peace with a spouse or parent. Thus we stood at San Miguel in common need, slowly building a bond leading to an acceptance of each other that, indeed, is what Christ taught.

Not that everyone at San Miguel liked each other. I was there long enough to know of some of the divisions, differences, and disagreements that exist (I had some of them myself). So the people of San Miguel are people, but they do try to love each other with the real love of Christ. The best definition of this love that I have found is in the book *The Road Less Traveled* by M. Scott Peck. He defines love as work and courage. This is the love I saw in action at San Miguel.

There were many times that I felt loved at San Miguel. From being accepted in a pew that first time I went to Mass, to being accepted into family gatherings at *matanzas*[32] and Christmas Eves, the people of San Miguel opened their hearts and homes to this Anglo student. They also accepted me into the Saturday evening choir.

The choir was the counterbalance to graduate school that got me through the long years of study and the stress of writing a thesis. The choir brought me into the life of San Miguel. I was involved with the planning of liturgies and saw all that went on preparing for Masses. I was in the sacristy bustling with activity. I was in the front of the church during Mass where I could see what was going on — even the unplanned and the funny. More than once I shook with stifled laughter. The choir helped me become a part of the place and let me contribute. The crowning moment of my time there was when I chanted the Easter Proclamation on Holy Saturday 1989. I had wanted to sing it for all the years I had been there, but Paul was the better singer and always got to do it. I fought a lot with the monster of jealousy in the Easter choir and poor Sister Rosie was a saint to put up with me. But finally, the Easter after I had moved to New York, I returned to finish my Ph.D. thesis and got to sing it. As I looked out on the congregation I knew that people loved me there and that even if I blew the singing completely they would be kind to me and accept me as one of them. They had already done so many times as I, without training or experience, learned to express my need and my love for God in song. When I can pray no other way, I sing, because that is how I prayed at San Miguel. There were many times when

---

32. A *matanza* is when a pig is killed and butchered. People are invited over to make it a party and to share the immense amount of work.

I was not worth listening to, but people were always kind. There were also times when people told me that they were touched by my singing. I knew even then that though it was me that sang, it was God that touched them. I am grateful to have been able to serve as the messenger.

After I sang the Easter Proclamation I went back to the VLA office and completed the final copy of my thesis. At 4:20 a.m. on that Easter morning I stacked the three required copies on my advisor's desk and was finished, at long last, with graduate school, but not with Socorro. That community held me close, and it has not been easy to leave. A year and a half after finishing my thesis I sat watching the luminarias in the earliest hours of a frigid Christmas day. Many images of the inside of San Miguel Church filled my mind. I have been in that church when it was filled to capacity and overflowing on Ash Wednesday. I have stood shoulder to shoulder in the choir on Christmas and Easter. I have also been there alone in the light and in the dark facing God and myself. I have sung in large choirs, I have sung alone, and I have been silent, unable to express what is in my heart. In that church my heart has known some of its greatest joys and its darkest despair. I have hugged and cried, loved and hated in that church (yes, there were some truly dark moments for me there when conflict made life there a struggle). All in all I have lived in that church and it has been the center of the life of my heart and soul. While my mind struggled to learn of the universe and radio astronomy, my heart and soul struggled with following Christ, with loving, forgiving, and seeking God. And God is very close to San Miguel.

When I think of San Miguel, I always think of the sound of the door softly closing as people quietly gather for the morning Mass. That sound is the sound of a place where I belonged with all my flaws because others aware of their own flaws accepted me. It was not unusual for there to be a coffin in the side chapel, or the lingering scent of incense from a funeral the previous day. There, in the morning, before the "everydayness" of the day took over, people pause at San Miguel to open their hearts and their awareness to things greater than themselves. The people there are at ease with a coffin in the room because in the pause of every morning they think of death as a part of this mystery of life, and this church embraces life.

After an hour and a half I got too cold to stay outside with the luminarias any longer. As I took my long last look, I realized that I have truly been a part of San Miguel and, by that, it has become a part of me. I carry San Miguel with me wherever I go because I carry the love that I knew there and the tolerance for myself that I learned there. As I picked up my stool to go inside and walked past the luminarias lining the sidewalk I realized that those little fires must glow within me, even in New York, to guide the pilgrims I meet toward the San Miguel in my own heart where God dwells.

Chapter 10

A God to Match
My Universe

DID GOD CREATE the universe? That's primary in many people's definition of God, but as a scientist, I must admit that I'm not sure. The way I express this is that I can't decide what the Venn diagram of the universe and God is. It could be any of five: God and the universe completely separate, God and the universe mostly separate with a small overlap, the universe contains God, God contains the universe or God and the universe are co-extant, as illustrated on the next page.

Of these, I mostly operate on the last two, that the universe is contained by God and, perhaps, created by God, or they are co-extant. Sometimes, I tend toward the middle one where the universe contains God. I do not believe either of the first two, where they are completely separate or where great chunks of the universe and God exist separate from each other. Some of the other believing scientists I know seem to operate under the first two diagrams by compartmentalizing their science and their faith. This is the "science and faith are in different realms" attitude, where the only intersection between them may be within the human person. That has never sat well with me. I believe it has to be a single, coherent universe, simply because I believe I'm a single, coherent being. Within me, the physical and the spiritual are integrated into one person so I believe they have to be integrated in the universe and not separated into realms.

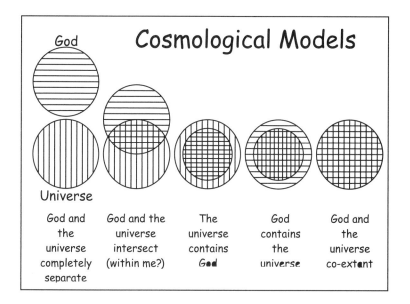

Operating on the last two diagrams doesn't require God to have created the universe, but it does require that the universe — its spacetime continuum filled with matter-energy and all the weird-nesses and wonders — is filled with God and expresses the mind, the creative imagination, and/or the very nature of God. In his lectures in *The Divine Dance*,[33] Richard Rohr quotes Catherine LaCugna's *God for Us,* where she comes at this same conclusion from the theology of the Trinity, saying, "Whatever is happening in God cannot be just an inner, hidden secret. It has to be reflected in the outer universe."[34]

Most, if not all believers sense God's presence in the beauty of sunsets, star-filled skies, snow-capped mountains, and fields of wild-flowers. I sense God in these things, too. But I also sense God in the

---

33. Richard Rohr, *The Divine Dance: Exploring the Mystery of the Trinity,* available from the Mustard Seed at the Center for Action and Contemplation, Albuquerque, New Mexico (www.cacradicalgrace.org/).

34. Catherine LaCugna, *God for Us: The Trinity and Christian Life* (San Francsico: HarperSanFrancisco, 1993).

vastness, the weirdness, the abundance, the seeming nonsensicalness, and even the violence of this incredible universe.

At last count, there were hundreds of billions of galaxies, each made up of hundreds of billions of stars with their attendant planets, moons, asteroids, and comets. These stretch in net-like archipelagos over space so vast that the light we receive from the most distant galaxies has been traveling at 186,000 miles per second for over 13 billion years. A God present to this vastness and who perhaps created it, must be so "other" that, like Job I am reduced to covering my mouth in recognition that anything I speak of this God falls far short of the reality.

As I write this, I am surrounded by light and matter — things so common that we rarely consider their weirdness. The light entering my eyeball behaves as a wave as it refracts in the lens and focuses on my retina. But for me to detect it and see these words appearing on the screen as I type, the particle nature of light must arise as small packets of energy interacting with the cells of my rods and cones communicating the colors of the screen with their energies and its brightness by their number. Each time I save the file on my USB Flash drive, electrons must act as waves to tunnel through energy barriers turning millions of tiny switches on or off to store these words as binary code. Matter and energy are two expressions of the same cosmic stuff with a fundamental nature that is both a particle and a wave. Matter and energy are everything we know in the universe. So everything in the universe, at its deepest level, exists as two contradictory natures at the same time. What does this say about God?

Teilhard de Chardin wrote of this when he said, "The essential marvel of the divine milieu is the ease with which it assembles and harmonizes within itself qualities which appear to us to be contradictory."[35] So what might be the "wave particle duality" of God? There

---

35. Pierre Teilhard de Chardin, *The Divine Milieu* (New York: Harper & Row, 1960), 113.

are many possibilities. Within Christianity, Jesus' natures as God and human seem a perfect equivalent. More broadly, perhaps the "no God" of Buddhism and the personal God of Christianity express a sort of wave-particle duality: God so transcendent, so "other" as to be beyond personality or even "being," at the same time that God is so immanent so as to speak and love within us. In view of the reality that light and matter are incomprehensible, it follows that any God of this universe must be just as incomprehensible.

As baffling as the vastness and weirdness of the universe, is the abundance of it. The sun converts a mass of hydrogen equivalent to 62 aircraft carriers to helium every second. 0.7 percent of that mass is converted to energy, yielding the equivalent of 3.8 septillion 100-watt light bulbs in energy. And it has done this fairly constantly for over 4 billion years. Of this vast amount of energy, 1,370 watts has fallen on every square meter[36] of Earth's atmosphere for all that time. With the current atmosphere (which took about 2 billion years to evolve), an average of 51 percent of that energy reaches the ground. With the sun directly overhead, that's about 700 watts falling on the ground. Across the days, latitudes, and seasons, this ranges down to zero, but it's still a huge amount of energy that has sustained almost all of life on Earth, and certainly each one of us through the plants' conversion of this energy to the sugars and carbohydrates that feed us.

As incredible as the sun's energy is, it's not the only source of energy for life on Earth. In deep trenches of the ocean, entire ecological communities thrive in complete darkness, deriving their life from black smokers, superheated water rich in energy and mineral nutrients emerging from deep within the Earth. The source of heat for this water is leftover heat from the planet's violent formation and heat generated by radioactive decay of heavy elements; the same radioactivity that is so toxic to life gives life to these creatures. The heat of Earth's interior keeps Earth a living planet for all of us by

---

36. Actually, every square meter perpendicular to the sun.

continuously generating the magnetic field that protects the atmosphere and surface from the deadly radiation of particles from the sun and galaxy. We only sense the magnetic field when using a compass to find our way or when auroral displays light up the sky. Next time you have the privilege of watching the incredible dancing rays of the northern or southern lights, recognize them as the active boundary between the benefit and danger of radioactivity.

On the surface of Earth, life exists and even flourishes everywhere, powered by the same sun from whose harmful radiation and particles the magnetic field and atmosphere protect us while allowing its beneficial radiation to power all we know. In the dry valleys of Antarctica, bacteria live within the rocks. Bacteria also live in boiling mud and water in Yellowstone National Park and other geothermally active regions. In more hospitable environments, the profusion of life is mind-numbing. The sheer abundance of forests, grasslands, oceans, and even deserts can overwhelm me with wonder.

Along with the abundance, the seeming nonsensicalness of some creatures inclines me toward believing that a God of generous love and a wry sense of humor does somehow influence creation. I would never call it "design" since I don't believe God plans or even knows what may emerge from the random processes of physics, chemistry, and biology. Yet I do sense God's delight in what does emerge and a sense of God's influence in the emergence of some incredibly delightful creatures. Things like insects and reptiles seem to me to be the "sensible" life forms that would emerge. But why would any universe come up with puppies? I imagine that someday biologists and paleontologists will be able to map out the few-hundred-million-year-process of Proterozoic pond scum evolving into puppies, and I have no doubt it will be perfectly reasonable, not requiring any suspension of the standard laws of science and not requiring any belief in God. For one who believes in God, though, it's hard not to see God winking at us with the eyes of puppies. A way of saying that God exists, God delights in the creatures of Earth, the universe is ultimately friendly, life is a fleeting adventure, and we might as well have fun.

To honor the puppies as windows to the delight of God, I am on a personal campaign to change the name of a group of puppies from a "litter" (who could ever think of puppies as litter?) to an "exuberance." This expresses their nature as do the names of an exaltation of larks and a murder of crows. I invite you, dear reader, to join me on this campaign and start using the term to get it into common usage. It can refer to a group of related puppies so that one could say, "Our dog gave birth to an exuberance of puppies last night. They are all so cute!" It can also refer to an unrelated group of puppies as in "Wow, did you see the exuberance of puppies in the *Animal Planet* Puppy Bowl this year?"

However, one can't study the universe without becoming deeply aware of its danger and violence. On Earth, earthquakes, tsunamis, and volcanic eruptions have killed millions of people and billions of other creatures. These arise because the surface we find so solid, *terra firma,* is actually a thin crust, equivalent to the thickness of a postage stamp on a basketball, that heaves and buckles from the churning of Earth's molten interior. This is the same molten interior to which we owe the protective magnetic field. It seems every benefit also threatens us.

In about 5 billion years, as it begins to run out of fuel, the sun will swell to engulf Mercury, Venus, and perhaps even the Earth. The star that has powered life on Earth will then destroy it as its intensity increases with its size, evaporating the oceans, desiccating the landscape and ablating the atmosphere in spite of the protective magnetic field. At its death, it will explode as a planetary nebula, like the ring nebula in Lyra. At that point it will likely ablate the Earth itself, blasting back into interstellar space the elements of which we are made. Everything we are will return to the stars and perhaps get incorporated into another star-forming nebula.

Giant stars die in supernovae, more spectacular explosions than planetary nebulae. If one were to occur within a couple of hundred light years of the Earth, the radiation would severely harm life on its surface. This may have happened in geologic time and as recently as 2 million years ago, when *Homo erectus* was migrating from Africa to other continents. The evidence for this is an isotope of iron, ^{60}Fe, with 34 neutrons (and 26 protons) and a half-life of 1500 years found in cores taken from the ocean floor.[37] The only place to create this iron is in supernovae, so one must have occurred close enough to Earth for this fallout to blanket our planet. The layer corresponds to a large-scale extinction of marine mollusks, perhaps victims of the supernova. Among our ancestors, there may also have been sickness and death as ^{60}Fe and other toxic, radioactive elements coated the Earth. And yet we could not exist without the products of supernovae. Iron and all heavier elements can be created only in supernovae. We would have no iron to carry oxygen in our bloodstream, no nickel to mix into our coins, no copper for our pipes and wires, no iodine to regulate our metabolisms, no silver, no gold, no mercury or lead if the interstellar cloud from which the sun formed had not been enriched by the fallout from a supernova. In fact, a supernova near the cloud may have triggered the formation of the sun. We owe our existence to supernovae — and yet they are lethal.

On the Earth, the very processes maintaining the environment that supports life, the sunlight, the weather, the radioactivity of the deep interior, are dangers. Sunlight causes cancer; lightning, tornados, and hurricanes kill thousands of people and animals every year; volcanoes, earthquakes, and tsunamis threaten and kill many more.

This juxtaposition of benefit and tragic violence is made most stark to me by roadkill. Many days as I drive the ten miles between my job and home, beautiful, wondrous creatures have been reduced to heaps of fur and smears of blood and bone. I am deeply saddened by the sight of each one of these animals; the deer, raccoons, porcupines, skunks, squirrels, and even pet cats and dogs. I always think about the scampering creature it was before it was hit by a speeding car whose driver may not even have taken notice of the impact. I pray that they

---

37. *New Scientist*, 2002 (*www.newscientist.com/article.ns?id=dn1764*).

did not suffer as they lay in the road alone, dying of their injuries. Sometimes I will stop and move a body out of the roadway onto a patch of earth or grass to prevent it from being further battered. More often, it is already off the roadway, and I'm in too much of a rush to stop, but it touches me deeply and brings me up against one of the great conundrums of the spiritual journey: the juxtaposition of blessing and curse.

I certainly see my car as a blessing. The metals were forged in supernova explosions before the sun and planets formed from an interstellar cloud. Those metals were dug from the Earth by human labor and formed into an automobile by human intelligence and skill. My car allows me a personal freedom and mobility that I cherish and delight in. But the processes of building my car scar and pollute the land and water. Driving my car pollutes the atmosphere as does the building and maintaining of the roads that pollute the land and the water. The roads also create dangerous barriers for wildlife, pets, and people. The dead creatures beside the road remind me of all these costs to the benefit of my zipping down the road singing along with Enya's "Sail Away"[38] and brings me to reflective silence. I feel help-less against the animal's suffering and death. All I can do, trivial and unhelpful as it seems, is to acknowledge it so that this one creature's death does not pass unnoticed. I also raise a prayer for the spirit continuing on its journey, wherever that may be. But the sadness remains as a stone in the shoe of my soul, confronting me with dis-comfort at random moments when I would otherwise be on autopilot and forcing me to contemplate the relationship between the loving intelligence I sense as God and the random, often violent physical universe.

Teilhard de Chardin acknowledged the juxtaposition of benefit and violence in the "Mass on the World," which he wrote on a sci-entific expedition (he was a paleontologist) to the Ordos desert in Inner Mongolia in 1923. Since he had "neither bread, nor wine, nor

---

38. Available on *Enya's Watermark* CD (Reprise Records, 1989).

altar,"[39] the regular implements for offering Mass, he raised himself "beyond these symbols, up to the pure majesty of the real, itself"[40] and offered God all the "labours and sufferings of the world." At the consecration, where the bread and wine become the body and blood of Christ, Teilhard says, "Do you now therefore, speaking through my lips, pronounce over this earthly travail your twofold efficacious word.... Over every living thing which is to spring up, to grow, to flower, to ripen during this day say again the words: This is my Body. And over every death-force which waits in the readiness to corrode, to wither, to cut down, speak again your commanding words which express the supreme mystery of faith: This is my Blood."[41] Teilhard goes farther than simply acknowledging the violence of the universe, but encourages us to embrace it as part of the nature of God as he says, "Bathe yourself in the ocean of matter; plunge into it where it is deepest and most violent; struggle in its currents and drink of its waters. For it cradled you long ago in your preconscious existence; and it is that ocean that will raise you up to God."[42]

If God is knitted into the fabric of this universe, what does the violence and danger say about God? When disasters occur, we often hear from survivors that it was "God's will." Does God actually will disasters upon us or could it be that the very vitality of this universe requires violent processes that God will not or cannot stop? I don't believe God wills animals to dart into the paths of cars, nor does God will tornados and tsunamis into existence and aim them at particular towns or cities. But I also do believe that God does not prevent or stop them because it would endanger the very wonder of existence. Also, I'm not sure God has the power to stop them. Can God suspend physical laws? If the fourth Venn diagram at the beginning of this chapter is accurate, if God created the universe and decided the laws

---

39. Pierre Teilhard de Chardin, *Hymn of the Universe* (New York: Harper & Row, 1965), 19.

40. Ibid.

41. Ibid., 23.

42. Ibid., 65.

of physics, I suppose that God can suspend physical law. Since I can't decide among the Venn diagrams, I remain skeptical of God's power to do this. Moreover, I remain skeptical of God's need, or desire, or motivation to suspend physical law given the wonders of the stars, the Earth, and puppies that have emerged from the evolution of the universe in accord with these laws.

Chapter 11

Journey of
Desert Mornings

As the sky began to lighten toward dawn on the summer solstice, I would walk out to the center of the Very Large Array Radio Telescope to greet the dawn of midsummer's morning. As I walked, I knew that past the end of the north arm of the array, the monks and guests of the Monastery of Christ in the Desert were finishing the prayers of Vigils that began as I was leaving my home in Socorro hours earlier. In Socorro, the priest and members of the congregation were rising and preparing for the 7:00 a.m. Spanish Mass that I attended on the days I was not at the VLA site. As I looked up from the ancient lakebed on which I walked, the brilliant reds and oranges of the brightening sky silhouetted the twin domes of the Observatory for Cometary Research, where I had spent many a night taking long exposure photographs of comets. The observers would be starting their drive down the mountain with a stack of glass photographic plates carrying images of twists and kinks in dust and gas evaporated off the comet's surface by the same star whose rising I was preparing to witness.

Arriving at the center of the array, I stood in my own private *Antennahenge* as my Celtic forebears had stood amid standing stones to greet the dawn of the longest day. Around and through me, as the sky lightened visually, it was already bright in radio waves as it was throughout every day and night. Some of those radio waves had traveled across hundreds of millions or even billions of light-years[43]

---

43. A light-year is the distance light travels in a year. The speed of light is 186,000 miles/sec and a light-year is about 6 trillion miles.

of intergalactic space from the galaxies I had observed for my Ph.D. project as well as hundreds of billions of other galaxies. Though I could not sense the radio waves, I knew they were there and had even heard some of them as static from my radio tuned between stations.

Also beyond the reach of my physical senses, but sensed nonetheless by the tendrils of my heart and soul, knitted into all the physical wonders surrounding me, was a spirit that I could only name as God. This was not the Great White Father God of my Catholic childhood; this was a God who danced among the electromagnetic waves and gravitational ripples of intergalactic space and just as easily sat among the chanting monks or the congregation at morning Mass. There at the center of the array, my physical and spiritual worlds converged.

As the warming sun began its rise over the mountains, the brilliant reds and oranges bathing the few clouds of the New Mexico sky retreated to the west where the purple shadow of the Earth disappeared over the horizon on its endless journey. The sun's rays first illuminated the tops of the 92-foot-high antennas in dazzling white with only the merest hint of the yellow tint the atmosphere gives the light of our star. Slowly, the brilliance moved down along the antennas to reveal the grasses and cacti of the plains of San Augustin threaded by the railroad tracks of the array's three arms, along which the 230-ton antennas were moved every few months. Warmed by the sun, the rails expanded, clanging as they collided with each other. Radio astronomy's carillon greeting the dawn.

Behind me, inside the Science Library Office Building, fondly known as the SLOB, three computers were busy making millions of calculations to create images of distant galaxies from data I had obtained from the twenty-seven antennas of the array. With the dawn accomplished, I headed back to the computers to accomplish the work that had brought me to the array.

I had come to Socorro in the fall of 1981 to begin graduate school at New Mexico Tech. I had first sent an inquiry card to Tech in the summer after I graduated from Colorado Mountain College as a fling,

The Very Large Array at dawn.
Photo by Aileen O'Donoghue

not quite believing I'd ever actually pursue the Ph.D. in astrophysics that I had checked as my interest. Having discovered my calling to academic life later than most, I was dogged by a nagging sense that I wasn't really smart enough to accomplish my dreams. But there I was, a pre-doc fellow at the world's largest telescope spending every waking moment, and more than a few when I was asleep, analyzing radio data from eleven galaxies and seeking to understand the nature and environment of the radio-luminous plasma that rose, curled, and billowed across hundreds of thousands of light years.

Radio Astronomy

Radio waves, the ones that come from the radio station to the radio, not the sound waves from the radio to our ears, are produced quite easily by many physical systems where charged particles, most commonly electrons, are jiggled. Any acceleration of a charged particle produces a ripple in its electric field and creates a magnetic field that moves away from the particle at the speed of light as an electromagnetic wave. Shake staticky clothes out of the dryer and an electromagnetic wave races away. The frequency of the wave determined by its energy places it in the electromagnetic spectrum. Shake the clothes one hundred thousand times a second to broadcast in the AM band. Shake them 100 million times a second to broadcast in FM. The static heard between radio stations reveals the presence of radio signals from the natural and unnatural worlds. Much of the static is from distant radio stations, engines, garage door openers, remote car starters, and other technological devices. But some of it is from the sun, planets, other stars, and galaxies. Sorting out all the noise to obtain the signal from a single natural source is much of the work of radio astronomy.

Electrons in antennas and receivers detect the waves by jiggling in response to the changing electric and magnetic fields. This happens in the circuitry of the radio that then throws away the carrier wave and produces sound from the information encoded on the wave as small fluctuations in the amplitude or frequency (from which we get amplitude modulation, AM, or frequency modulation, FM).

The Very Large Array Radio Telescope has receivers tuned to frequencies in the FM band and higher. These waves are ten thousand times larger than the waves we detect as light so a larger instrument is needed to detect them. As an array, it acts as a zoom lens to shrink the portion of the sky from which it receives the strongest signals to less than an arc second, 1/3600th of a degree, a hundred-billionth of the area of the sky.

The array is shaped as a Y with the stem pointed north so that it looks upside down on a map. Along each arm of the array are pedestals on which nine antennas can be arranged to vary the resolution of the array, the area of the sky to which it is most sensitive. As with a zoom lens, there are situations that call for the wide field and those that require the greatest zoom. The array is varied between four configurations to accommodate these needs. At its most expanded, for the greatest zoom, the three arms stretch out thirteen miles from the center. The signal from each antenna is compared to that of each of the others so that the array acts as a single telescope twenty-six miles in diameter.

Using this instrument, I observed distant galaxies. In visible light they were fairly boring elliptical galaxies — large spheroidal, gravitationally bound globs of trillions of stars. In radio, however, our images showed jets and vast lobes of material streaming out from the galactic centers. What we saw shining with our radio telescopes were actually electrons caught in magnetic fields. Charged particles spiral in magnetic fields, following the lines of magnetic force. The particles of the solar wind are steered to Earth's magnetic poles by this effect, giving rise to the Aurora Borealis and Australis rarely seen from lower latitudes. As they spiral, the particles radiate electromagnetic waves that we can detect with our radio telescopes. I always took time to look at the antennas of the array when I knew they were observing one of my galaxies. As I did, I would try to comprehend the fact that electrons had jiggled a hundred million years ago, sending out radio waves that traveled across the universe. I would try to envision them crashing silently onto the New Mexico desert where electrons in receivers of the antennas pointed in their direction were jiggling in response to the ancient waves. The information from the electrons jiggling in the receivers then enabled this budding astronomer to create images of how the galaxies appeared in radio when the original electrons jiggled and life on Earth had barely advanced beyond pond scum. It felt as though my mind reached through the antennas across the vastness of space to touch a past more ancient than the desert floor on which I stood.

The images I created from the data showed jets of plasma from deep within the parent galaxy shooting out tens of thousands of light years where they suddenly disrupted into great plumes of material that seemed to be blown back in a wind of some sort. Others worked on figuring out the source of the plasma and concluded it to be the region around a supermassive black hole, thousands to millions of times more massive than the sun, where so much material was falling in toward it that some was squeezed out along the rotation axes of the galaxy like toothpaste being shot out of a tube.

What I studied about these galaxies was their interaction with their environment, specifically why the plumes bent. They reside near the centers of large clusters where thousands of galaxies are bound together by their mutual gravity. All the galaxies orbit the center of the cluster as planets orbit the sun, but the galaxies I studied were so near the center that their orbital motion was very slow compared to galaxies in the outer reaches. And yet the plumes of radio luminous plasma shooting out thousands of light-years from their nuclei bent and twisted like smoke in the wind where no wind should blow. Ultimately, work on these galaxies and their clusters showed that the clusters, themselves, were not settled collections of galaxies, but groups of sub-clusters, each surrounded by a vast halo of gas, colliding and interacting to eventually become a single giant cluster. Like the meetings of air masses that give rise to storms across the prairies as winter slowly yields to summer, the meeting of sub-cluster atmospheres give rise to "cluster weather" across vast reaches of space.

Very little of the work was as thrilling and romantic as watching the antennas observing my sources or greeting the dawn in the center of the array. Most of it was sitting in front of a computer terminal running the programs that created images from grids of snippets of electrical currents in each receiver compared with the snippets from all the others in a process called interferometry. The VLA was made possible only with the advent of computers and has continued to perform beyond expectations with every increase in computer technology. In the days I was there, the computers still filled entire rooms and all the astronomers competed for disk space. We never thought we'd fill our first 500 MB disk! My laptop now has more power than the combination of all the computers I used at the VLA, but they were impressive and powerful instruments in their day.

The program we used (and still use) to create the images is called the Astronomical Image Processing System, AIPS. The room where we worked at the terminals connected to the main image processing computers was, appropriately, the AIPS Cage, and the instructions for the program were collected in the *AIPS Cookbook* with an ape on its cover and an impressive collection of recipes for banana foods and beverages. I spent most of the hours of every day in this room for years. At one point, my friends became concerned that I was becoming vitamin D deficient because I was never out in sunlight — odd for a student in New Mexico! My Ph.D. thesis project required a great deal of image processing since I observed eleven galaxies in two frequency bands (1.5 GHz around 20 cm and 5 GHz around 6 cm) and four configurations (two for each frequency band to get the wide field and zoom images to combine). Early on in my work I realized that the astronomers at the VLA for a particular observing project (on an "observing run") tended to work until 3:00 or 4:00 a.m. and the astronomers permanently on staff tended to come in around 10:00 a.m. This left a window between 4:00 and 10:00 in the morning when the computers were being used very little. That window became my time to work. With night-owl tendencies up to that point, it was sheer will power and need that got me out of bed at 3:00 a.m. But I came to love and feel very much at home in the predawn world I discovered. On the days when I taught at New Mexico Tech in Socorro, I would rise before 5:00 a.m. to run and attend the 7:00 a.m. Spanish Mass. On the days when I went to the VLA, I began my fifty-mile drive west to the observatory by 4:00 a.m. When I visited the monks of the Monastery of Christ in the Desert, I rose with them at 4:00 a.m. to chant psalms, meditate, and pray as the walls of Chauma cañon emerged from darkness into day.

What I learned in those desert mornings, though I was most often alone, was the fundamental reality that seeking truth about the universe and our existence in both science and faith requires individual effort and honesty, but also requires community. Although one can, and usually does, do experiments and observations alone in a lab or observatory, for one's work to become *science*, it has to be brought out to the scientific community as a paper in a refereed journal. It's not *science* until other scientists have vetted the methods, the data, and the conclusions. Similarly, the journey of faith, the honest and deep search for truth, also requires community. Though our experiences in prayer and meditation are private, the hard work of separating experience from fantasy and enlightenment from egotism requires bringing our experience out and learning of the experiences of others. Not that religious or spiritual experiences can be vetted the way scientific data can, but it is so easy for us to fool ourselves that we cannot accept them as truth without some examination. Those that do can become their own gods and do great harm to themselves and others.

Chapter 12

The Darkness

MY PILGRIMAGE was not to a place, but to a time. It was a pilgrimage to this hour before dawn where I sit with the monks of the Monastery of Christ in the Desert. My back grows cold against the adobe chapel wall that holds the chill of the northern New Mexico winter even into this last week of May. The monks are silent. The oil lamps, dimmed for meditation, do not overcome the darkness, but reveal its presence among us, resting in the folds of cowls and blue jeans. Sinking into meditation, eyes close, heads bow, and minds' eyes turn inward seeking the light of the spirit. But I cannot close my eyes. Instead, my face turns skyward. I look out through the tall, high windows to the stars of Cygnus, shining bright against the Milky Way, which glitters in the moonless sky. Twilight has not yet begun and past the stars of our galaxy, 16 billion light-years of darkness stretch from the monastery chapel to the primal fires of the Big Bang. Those fires yet shine, but at frequencies my eyes cannot see. To my eyes, the primal fires have gone out, leaving the universe dark and cold. That cold darkness floods down from the sky to this chapel, where it becomes the companion of this silent community. We are at home here in the peace of these hours when most sleep, some work, but monks and astronomers thrive, immersed in mysteries obscured by the light.

Finding my home in the darkness was not easy. Before I knew the depth of the sky I saw it as a bespeckled roof that dazzled me with its beauty. The patterns of the stars, in rhythm with the seasons, were comfortable friends that made every place from which I viewed them familiar. I sought to know more of them by studying astronomy. I did not know when I began that one's intellect cannot travel without one's spirit and that my intellectual journey to the cosmos would carry my soul to a vast darkness in which it would have to find a home. As I learned of science I soon found myself struggling with the loss of assumptions I did not know I'd held.

On a cold Rocky Mountain night, I discovered that my universe of stars did not need God. In the despair that followed, I learned that I had believed in God only because I could find no other way to create the universe. In learning of the chemistry and evolution of life and the processes of stars, my need for the creative power of God diminished. Stars shine by nuclear fusion. Amino acids float in interstellar space. Life evolves slowly and erratically through accidents of mutation and environmental pressure. As I became aware of the number and complexity of processes explained by application of the simple laws of physics and chemistry, my belief in God was peeled away like the layers of an onion. As my knowledge of science grew, so did my confidence that the universe was ultimately simple and comprehensible. What science did not yet know, it would figure out. Magic need not be invoked to explain anything. The onion had no core. Even the fact that some things may never be known does not mean that something supernatural had to happen. Just because we can't (yet) explain it doesn't mean that God had to do it. Ultimately, every cosmology comes down to a belief in something that has either always existed or come to be out of nothing. Since the universe does exist, one of them has to be true, but neither is easy to believe, whether you call it God or physics.

In my acceptance of physics, it seemed that I had recast my soul. The metal of science — based on reproducible results, logic, and the harmonic, intricate patterns of the universe — melted and replaced the tenuous layers of candle wax, incense, and memorized prayers that my belief in God had been. I hadn't known what comfort that belief had given me until, knee deep in snow, I looked out to the stars and saw only stars. I realized that I could conceive of a universe without God. As a student of astronomy, I felt that if the universe does not need God, I could not invoke God's existence without compromising my integrity as a scientist. That night the metal of my soul took on the cold of the snow and the ache of profound existential aloneness from which my belief in both God and God's love had protected me. The universe was reduced to the vast darkness that is its physical substance and I found it profoundly empty and lonely.

Mine was a scientist's universe: naked, honest, unadorned with the comforting myths of religion. I saw the myths as being for the ignorant and those without the courage to face reality. To be a scientist, I thought, I had to face it with painful honesty. This I did, and sought comfort in the assurance of my intellectual superiority. But the sky haunted me. From my observatory in the Magdalena mountains I gazed deep into the night with my eyes and with my telescopes while my heart turned away and hid.

The star Alberio, shining in the dark, silent sky, slips slowly from one window pane to the next as Earth carries the canyon of the Chauma River to face the sun. The cantor turns up his lamp and begins to sing. His voice blends with the darkness and mingles the mysteries of humanity with those of the cosmos. His chant infuses the physical darkness with the spiritual darkness that has called me here and now calls me back from the stars. I turn to the psalmody in my lap to chant of pain, of fear, of defeat, of triumph, of love, and of humanity reaching out to God. In two choirs exchanging silence and song we express our tenuous sense of something beyond ourselves that unites us with each other and with the cosmos shining through the windows. In the songs and the silence we express our longing to touch this presence.

My mind leaped to touch the universe even as my heart hid from the dark. On the plains of San Augustin, radio signals that had traveled for hundreds of millions of years crashed silently into a field of antennas. There the ancient songs of electrons caught in magnetic fields were received as tiny electric currents that, amplified, combined, cut into data bits, and Fourier-transformed yielded images of galaxies with jets of radio-luminous plasma bending and twisting in cosmic winds where no winds should blow. The more I learned of the universe, the less I knew, and the more fascinating and complex it became. I lived with a deep awareness of the profound wonders beyond the blue New Mexico sky and slowly recognized that it is through the tiny gaps where our predictions disagree with our results only very slightly that nature teaches us of quantum mechanics and chaos and slips in the wonders of starlight and thunderstorms. The universe is a much weirder place than we and our theories would ever expect it to be. And the weirdest thing I know is me, a child of the universe with my heart hiding from the night.

Because the night is my home. The very elements of my flesh and bones were forged in the cores of stars. The hydrogen bound in the water that makes up most of my substance is only a tenth of a millisecond younger than the universe itself. I am, as Carl Sagan put it, "the matter of the cosmos, contemplating itself." In my heart beats the pulse of stars, galaxies, and clouds of cold hydrogen. And I know it. And it is my knowing that I know that forms the gap between my experience of existence and my knowledge of the physical universe through which God, to my startled and joyful surprise, emerged from the exile imposed by a younger, less knowledgeable, less confident and open scientist. The universe does not need God, but if it is weird enough to contain me, it might just be weird enough to contain, or be contained, by God.

Twilight begins. The stars continue to slip past the window panes. The high eastern walls of the canyon, visible only by the starlight they block, slowly reveal the constellation of Andromeda. As we conclude our prayers, the light of our own star scattering through the blanket of the atmosphere will leave the more distant stars, like our morning prayers, in our memories and our hearts.

This God that slipped into my universe is very different than the one I banished. My childhood God was rulebound and manipulated by candles and incense. For the price of ten Our Fathers, He would forgive all the school-skipping, brother-fighting, bad-word-saying, and cigarette-sneaking sins of a childhood week — and wouldn't really expect me to be different the next week. Such a God could not slip through a gap in cosmology. Indeed, such a God could not admit the existence of a gap in cosmology. The God that did slip through seems to know nothing of rules, but continually casts me adrift in my own freedom while stuffing wonders in the gaps between what we expect the universe to contain and what we find. Black holes arise from stellar explosions, falcons nest on skyscrapers, Francis of Assisi emerges from wealth, and Gandhi and King emerge from prejudice and oppression. It is in the unexpected, yet very ordinary wonders of nature and people that call me to believe in God, and "God" is my name for the creative source of the abundance of the universe that arises in the human soul as love.

My heart has emerged from where it hid slowly, cautiously, fearing that this God of abundance and love is another myth that my intellect will reject and send back through a closing gap in my scientific universe. But I am awash in the abundance of the universe. It shouts at me from the night sky, the Earth, and my own soul. The vast darkness of space is not empty but is filled with the electromagnetic songs of electrons while its very fabric is rippled by gravity waves sent out by the orbital ballets of giant stars. And in this obscure corner of space, the warm, green, tropical sea casts billions of shells upon the shore, each one a life's product. Wading in the sea as the sun sets, I rejoice at the wonders of the sky and sea from which I emerged to sit in a monastery chapel.

In a shaft of sunlight, the stream of incense smoke curls in the eddy left by the monk's passing cowl. As it rises to the light, a symbol of our prayers rising to God, it spirals, disappearing as it passes into the shadows cast by the window frames, then emerging again into the light. I sit in the sun on the same stool where I rested in the darkness of the morning. My chill dispelled by sunlight and coffee, I am immersed in the warmth of the community of monks and guests at prayer. Watching the incense smoke spiral, I see the path of my life as it moves from light to darkness and back again, rising in ever growing circles toward the God of light who is also God of the darkness.

Chapter 13

Science, Faith, and Community

THERE ARE TWO MANTRAS I constantly recite to my students. The first is that science is the current best guess; the second is that you can't do science in your basement. You can do experiments in your basement on the isolated mountaintop laboratories where the "mad scientists" of cartoons and horror movies work, but to do *science*, you have to present your methods, data, and conclusions to the scientific community so that others can reproduce your results.

Science as the current best guess means that we can never be certain that our theories are correct. A theory is actually a model of the universe, and since a model is never the thing it represents, the most we can say is that the data are consistent with our theories. The universe is consistent with our theories, but our theories are not the universe. The map can never be the territory, no matter how accurate. Thus nothing in science is ever fully "proved." All theories remain theories and are constantly tested against nature through experiments and observations. To say that all science knows is theories, however, does not in any way mean that science knows nothing! A theory is not something that popped into someone's mind yesterday; that's a hunch. It's not even something that has some theory and even rough data to go with it; that's a hypothesis. In spite of our everyday usage of the word "theory" as an untested idea, in science a theory is well supported with logic or math from other established theories and experimental data. Some argue against the teaching of evolution because it's "only a theory."

How distressed those individuals might be to know that the "laws" of Newton that have governed our spacecraft traveling across the solar system and the "laws" of Kirchhoff governing all our electronic circuits are also theories. Granted they have much better predictive power than evolution since they model much simpler systems, but they are and will always remain theories. New and unexpected ideas or data often change or even overturn theories.

Albert Einstein's theory of special relativity showed that Newton's laws, where time and space are measured identically by different observers, don't apply when the observers' speeds with respect to each other approach the speed of light. His theory of general relativity showed that Newton's law of gravity does not fully explain gravity. In particular, the fact that gravity slows the passage of time is completely missing from Newton's "law." More recently, observers were profoundly startled when data from supernovae in distant galaxies showed that the universe's expansion is not slowing as predicted, but accelerating, changing the theory of the Big Bang in an unexpected way. New data and new insights can always change our models of the universe so science is always our current best guess.

The fact that you can't do science in your basement shows that science is an endeavor of the human community. Individuals seeking to contribute to science are required to learn the current understanding of the community before contributing their own ideas. This is done primarily in the process of earning academic degrees and acquiring credentials. Once scientific work is done, it must be published in a refereed journal where others in the specialty must approve the methods and conclusions to qualify the work for publication.

Conspiracy theorists claim that the refereeing process is in place to keep science orthodox, but the true function of it is to keep science as honest as any human endeavor can be and keep it on the path to truth about the universe. Through this process, science seeks to be self-correcting. If someone does publish fraudulent data or an incorrect conclusion, other researchers seeking to reproduce or expand upon the work will discover the fraudulence or errors. When cases of fraud in science are uncovered, I am sometimes challenged by people about the supposed honesty of scientific reporting of data. My response to the challenge is that the very fact that the fraud was discovered and exposed is evidence that the scientific process is working as it should. Every person, even a highly respected scientist, is capable of fraud, particularly when the data challenge expectations.

At the research frontiers of science, where measurements are precise and limits in instrumental accuracies accounted for, results that don't fit expectations are suspect. The first reaction is that the data are incorrect. It's much easier to think you screwed something up than that your experiment has revealed something unexpected! The temptation to "fix" the data, particularly when your funding depends on it, arises in all of us. In a few, out of fear they'll lose their funding or an inability to think their theory is flawed, fixing the data seems to be the right thing to do. Such data may get past referees into publication, but it's likely that some alert researcher trying to reproduce their work will discover the fraudulence and bring it to the attention of the scientific community. That's how the process is supposed to work and, over the long term, it does. An error in Newton's *Principia* published in 1687 was not discovered until 1987,[44] so it can be a long process!

The evidence that the process is not to maintain orthodoxy is the number of times unpopular theories challenging the deep assumptions of scientists have come to be accepted. Johannes Kepler, considered to be the first "astrophysicist," who devoted his life to figuring out the motions of the planets, was forced by the data to accept a reality he found abhorrent: that planets orbit the sun in ellipses, not perfect circles. Without the tools of calculus or calculators, he did long and tedious calculations of planetary positions. Kepler's God was a geometer and he believed Aristotle's view that the heavens, the abode of God, were perfect. A geometer God would

---

44. Robert Garisto, a senior at the University of Chicago, discovered that Newton had used 11 instead of 10.5 for the angle between a line from the sun to the center of the Earth and one to its surface (see Garisto, *American Journal of Physics* 59 [1991]: 42–48).

have the planets move in perfect circles. Kepler used mathematics to construct models of the orbits of the planets and compared the predictions to those observed by the greatest astronomer of the day, Tycho Brahe. At his observatory, he was able to measure the positions of celestial objects to an accuracy of 1 minute of arc, 1/60th of a degree. Until this time, the accuracy of observations had been limited to 10 minutes of arc. In calculations using circular orbits for Earth and Mars, Kepler's predicted positions differed from Tycho's observed positions by eight minutes of arc. Tiny as this seems to us, Kepler took it very seriously, stating, "Now, because they could not be disregarded, these eight minutes alone will lead us along a path to the reform of the whole of Astronomy, and they are the matter for a great part of this work."[45] The "reform of the whole of Astronomy" consisted of his three laws of planetary motion, the first of which is that the planets' orbits are ellipses, not circles, with the sun at one focus. However inconsequential this may seem to us, for Kepler it was disturbing in that it made God a rather crummy geometer!

Closer to our own time, the theories of Quantum Mechanics, the Big Bang, and Chaos have all disturbed the very scientists who discovered them. Einstein is said to have remarked about Quantum Mechanics that "God does not play dice," but eventually came to accept it as a powerful, if weird, model of the physical world of the very small.

Scientific data are objective and reproducible, yet we need the scientific community to keep science honest and, we hope, moving toward an accurate understanding of the universe. In the spiritual life, where the data are subjective and not reproducible at will, if at all, how can we keep ourselves honest and moving toward an accurate understanding of God? Just as science requires community, I believe the spiritual journey also requires community, though in quite a different way than refereed journals. First, unlike science, not all

---

45. From Kepler's work *Astronomia nova* (Heidelberg, 1609) chapter 19, 113–14 from www-gap.dcs.st-and.ac.uk/~history/Quotations/Kepler.html.

religions and not even all communities within a single religion agree
on the truth or the path to truth. I don't think this is an indication of
ultimate relativism, where everyone simply believes what they want
to, so much as it is an indication of the vastness and otherness of
God. Each community, due to cultural or historical differences, may
be sensitive to a different aspect of God. This doesn't mean that the
particular aspect of God to which any one of them is sensitive is
any less true than the others. The Dalai Lama addressed this at a
talk in Toronto in 2004.[46] He said that we must at the same time
believe there is one path and one truth for ourselves and that for the
great diversity of humankind (and animalkind for all we know; the
Buddhists seek the enlightenment of "all sentient beings") there are
many paths and many truths. Having to believe that all are true at
the same time that one is true seems impossible until I once again
remember that light is a particle and a wave at the same time.

It takes time, effort, travel and some risk to seek a community,
or perhaps just a small group of companions, with whom to share
the spiritual journey. It can be as destructive to associate with a
community that shares all of your ideas as one that shares none of
them. Recognizing that a community truly fostering spiritual growth
will neither be all comfort nor all discomfort has given me patience
with the nagging sense of fraudulence that can arise when I feel "out
of sync" with my parish, the Roman Catholic Church, or any group
of companions.

The communities I have known on my journey are the parishes
I've belonged to, the monks and guests at the Monastery of Christ
in the Desert, the sisters and companions of the Sisters of St. Joseph
of Concordia, Kansas, and the Jesuit Community of the Vatican
Observatory Research Group in Tucson, Arizona. Each of these communities shared some of their spiritual paths with me and I shared at
least some part of my spirituality with them.

---

46. The Dalai Lama participated in the Kalachakra for World Peace in Toronto, On-
tario, in which my sister, Kate, also participated. He also addressed an audience of
non-participants, where I heard him speak. See *www.ctao.org/kalachakra/*.

Parish Life

In the rituals and relationships with other believers, belief in a loving God seems sensible and less like brain damage or a character flaw than when I am around non-believers. It helps me to think that I'm not nuts for believing in God. In the twenty-five years I've been part of parishes, there have been seasons, times when I felt very connected to the parish and was heavily involved and times when I was minimally involved. Through all the years, though, my strongest link to the church has been weekday Mass.

The weekday Masses are much less of a production than those on the weekend. They are much more about quiet prayer and silence. There are a number of regulars who know each other and everyone's preferred pew. Now and then there's someone new who may be a transient, a visitor, or one who will join the regulars. For me, the great benefit of weekday Mass, particularly when I'm able to go often, is that it gives me pause to reflect on my spiritual life: what I am doing to grow in compassion and peacefulness. It can, and sometimes does become just another habit that I go though mindlessly, but still provides an opportunity, a venue, and a community to connect with God.

My current parish in New York is St. Mary's. It is in the Diocese of Ogdensburg, which is mostly rural, with only the two small cities of Watertown and Plattsburgh lending any hint of urban experience. It's also a quite conservative, mostly white diocese. I can struggle with the conservatism, but even here I have found surprisingly open and thoughtful people and programs. In 1993 I started the two-year Formation for Ministry program offered by the diocese. It was a two-year program of weekly two-hour academic classes on topics such as scripture, spirituality, sacraments, and moral theology. I was thrilled to finally find an opportunity to engage with religion at an intellectual level and loved the program. I was commissioned a lay minister in the diocese in 1995.

My need for spiritual community, though, is not entirely satisfied by my parish. I want opportunities to go deeper, to confront myself and seek God with more intensity than weekday Mass in the midst of daily life can provide.

Chanting with Monks

Soon after I had joined the church in Socorro, I read an article in the *Rocky Mountain News* about the Monastery of Christ in the Desert and was entranced by photos of its adobe chapel. I wrote them asking if I could "make a retreat" among them, not really knowing what that meant! They replied that they had accommodations for guests and it was not terribly expensive,[47] so I went to explore a place that would become "spiritual ground zero" for me for years.

I had never before visited a monastery or met a monk, but I drove up to Abiquiu, New Mexico, with great hopes. Across the street from Georgia O'Keeffe's Ghost Ranch, I turned onto the twelve-mile long dirt road that led to the monastery. Expecting to see it around every corner, when I finally did, I had a deep sense of being where I needed to be. By this time New Mexico had become my home and the adobe churches belonged there as though they had grown out of the very earth on which they stood. I parked at the gift shop and walked the quarter mile to the chapel, where a sign on a bell instructed guests to ring. I pulled the rope and the sound broke the silence so sharply I feared I had shattered the sky. Shortly Brother André appeared to give me a room and tell me I was free to join the monks at any or all services, but they did want to know if I was going to be at the main meal so they would know whether to set a place for me.

The room was tiny, perhaps ten feet square with a *bunco*, an adobe bench, on one wall with a camp mattress and bedding. There was a wardrobe and a desk with an oil lamp; only the kitchen and refectory had electric lights, powered by solar panels. There was also a small wood stove, the only source of heat. The very simplicity of the room gave me a deep sense of peace. It was truly a world away from the

---

47. They did not actually charge for lodging or meals, but stated what it cost the monastery to provide them and asked for whatever donation the guest could provide.

technological world of the radio observatory. Dinner was soup and bread eaten in silence with classical music from a cassette tape to mask the clatter of bowls and spoons. After supper were Vespers and Compline, the last community prayers of the day. At the end of Compline, the prior went around the chapel with a bundle of straw and bowl of water to bless every person there. So blessed and exhausted from the six-hour drive and darkness descending, I crawled into my narrow bed and slept.

It was still dark when the bells announced Vigils. I rose and made my way to the chapel. The chapel is in the shape of a Greek cross with equal sides. The inner square is topped by tall windows all around, allowing a view of the sky from every seat. From the path, the wavering light from the oil lamps emerged from those same high windows to create a warm glow that guided me through the dark. I arrived after the prayers had begun and instantly realized there was insufficient time to wait for the bells to wake me and that I'd have to use my travel alarm. The monks, undisturbed by my entrance, continued their chant. There were only rough, backless stools in the chapel with the choice ones against walls. Oil lamps were distributed so that the psalms could be read by all and all were invited to chant with the monks. Vigils lasted more than an hour. The night cold of the adobe wall at my back had sunk into me so I returned to my room and the warmth of my bed.

Through the days of that first stay, I learned and became comfortable with the rhythm of prayer and gentle pace of the day. There were work periods where guests would be assigned chores such as helping in the kitchen, folding laundry, splitting wood, washing windows, or other tasks. These were the times when the monks were most accessible, and through my years of visiting them, I learned they were mostly pretty normal guys seeking God. Not all were terribly holy, or articulate about their lives, but they all did seem authentic. An inauthentic monk probably wouldn't make it through a single winter!

Another important aspect of the monastery that appears in none of their brochures is the impact of the other guests. It was with the other guests that I was able to have deep conversations about the spiritual life and the work of keeping faith in the world. They were a select group, those who made their way to Christ in the Desert. Mostly they were older than me, well-educated liberal professionals with faith that had been inspired by the civil rights movement, Martin Luther King, the Berrigan brothers, and the four missionary women murdered in El Salvador. From our conversations, I learned much but, more importantly, gained confidence that one could be a well-educated professional and a practicing Catholic.

For all my attraction to the monastery, every time I went there it took me a day to settle; then contentedness would fill me. As the end of my time approached, though, my contentedness weakened and I found my mind returning to the world. Every time I left, I knew that I was not called to monastic life. My tendency to get deeply into projects for long hours makes the dividing up of the day by the set hours of prayer problematic. Also, having come of age during Watergate and Nixon's resignation, I don't believe I could ever trust any authority figure as much as the Rule of St. Benedict requires one to trust the superior. I also just don't like hierarchy. Though an organization may need someone designated to sign the checks, I operate much better in a team of equals than in a vertical structure. Perhaps that's why I chose the academy over the military! However, my love of the monastery remains, and I've found it valuable to incorporate some of the habits of silence, prayer, and work into my life with much help from Joan Chittister's *Wisdom Distilled from the Daily.*[48]

Companion of the Sisters of St. Joseph

There had been very few religious sisters, or nuns,[49] at Fitzsimons army parish. There were a few, but I didn't have to deal with them

---

48. San Francisco: HarperCollins, 1990.

49. Nuns are actually the equivalent of monks, living in monasteries. Most of the women called nuns are actually religious sisters. As an unapologetic geek, I have to use the correct, more awkward term.

at any depth and their strange costumes made me want to keep my distance. Thus the first sisters I got to know were Rosie and Carol at San Miguel. Since Rosie had responsibility for the folk choir and Newman group, we became close friends. She was from the C.S.J.[50] community in Concordia, Kansas, that had run St. Mary's Academy in Silver City, New Mexico, for many years. It was through Silver City that Rosie came to Socorro. She invited me to become a "Companion in Faith" with her community, a type of third order like the Dominican third order that Bob Hjellming belonged to. We traveled to Silver City for retreats and meetings a few times while I was in Socorro. San Miguel's youth minister, Bryan, was also a companion. On one trip with the three of us in the front seat of his pickup truck, we twisted the navy's "Join the Navy and see the world" to "Join the convent and see New Mexico."

The idea of joining a religious community stayed with me for many years. I was attracted to the companionship and the idea of not being so thoroughly on my own physically, emotionally, or spiritually. I met and became friends with many of the women of Concordia. After I had moved to New York and found myself driving across the country to tie my Colorado, New Mexico, and New York lives together without leaving QB behind,[51] I stopped in Concordia to spend a few days at Manna House, their retreat house, and felt very much at home. Later I would spend a weekend there on a "Come and See Retreat" for women considering religious life. Beverly, a woman in my group, did join the community. I could never figure out how to put my life as a professor in New York together with starting the process of joining the community. My job was too good to risk if I found I wasn't meant for religious community. Even if I could work out a leave of absence, I didn't have the financial resources to put my furniture, an inheritance from my grandmother (along with a fair

---

50. Congregation of St. Joseph, a different community from the S.S.J.s, the Sisters of St. Joseph.

51. I had flown her from Albuquerque to Denver and back once for Christmas and it was traumatic for her. She complained bitterly about the lack of a beverage service in baggage so I never forced her to fly again.

dose of chutzpa), in storage. I figured that if I were really called to religious life I would figure out how to do it. To this point, I have not figured it out, though I still find myself longing for it now and then.

Disturbing the Household:
A Year with the Vatican Observatory

I had heard of the Vatican Observatory, and even ventured to its website and looked for some of the staff at astronomy meetings, but I didn't have any idea how to connect with them. In January of 2000, though, I surfed the website of the Vatican Observatory Research Group (VORG). Among those who had been visitors at the observatory was someone I knew, an astronomer from Union College here in New York. Emboldened by this tenuous link, I emailed the webmaster, Chris Corbally, S.J., pictured with me on the cover of this book, about the possibility of spending my upcoming 2001–2 sabbatical leave from St. Lawrence with them. The next day I got a very positive response from the director of the observatory, George Coyne, S.J., saying they'd love to have me visit. George came to St. Lawrence to give the Niles Lecture on Science and Religion[52] the following fall, also visiting my astronomy class. One young man in my class was so amazed to have a priest, complete with a roman collar, discussing astronomy and religion without skipping a beat that he wrote me years after his graduation to tell me of its impact. He became neither an astronomer nor a priest, but from George's visit knew that science and religion could coexist without conflict.

During George's visit we discussed the details of my time in Tucson. St. Lawrence would be giving me half my usual salary which, with my rent, would cover my mortgage, taxes, and car payments, leaving me nothing to live on. The VORG couldn't pay me a salary. George asked what I needed in Tucson, and I told him I just needed to live there. He suggested they could give me room and board but

---

52. Supported by a grant from the family of Harold H. Niles, former chaplain of St. Lawrence University.

couldn't guarantee it. After he got back to Tucson and discussed it with the community, he let me know that "you will be welcome to reside in our Vatican Observatory community. I hope your friends won't desert you when they hear the word 'Vatican.' We have a bungalow just west of our main house. It has a roomy back yard and I think it would be the perfect place for you to be at peace with the doggies."[53] After a visit in March of 2001 to meet everyone and see what my living situation would be, I showed up on September 1, for a fascinating year.

When I say that I work with the "Vatican Observatory" I am often greeted by a puzzled "Isn't that an oxymoron?" since our culture is much more informed about Galileo's conflict with the church than about the true history of the church's relationship with science, including Pope Clement XI's ordering of seismological observations in 1703.[54] The Vatican Observatory can be dated back to 1582 when Pope Gregory XIII decided to reform the calendar. The Roman calendar is tied to the sun in that the Vernal (Spring) Equinox, when the sun crosses the equator moving north, should occur on or about March 21. This is important since the date of Easter is calculated as the first Sunday following the first full moon following the Vernal Equinox, fixed as March 21.[55] It is noteworthy that this date is still determined from tables and not actual astronomical observations of the equinox and full moon. In 1576, Gregory XIII commissioned the building of a 73 meter "Tower of the Winds" at Vatican City. It included a hole in the southern wall through which the sun would shine at noon. On the floor was a marble meridian line with a circle etched with the positions where the shaft of sunlight should fall on the equinoxes, solstices, and days when it enters the various signs of

---

53. QB "crossed the rainbow bridge" in 1998. Two of my students thought I was too sad without a dog so they brought Kiva (Kee'-va) into my life, and a year later, Dace (Da'-chay), the same mix as QB, joined our family.

54. Sabino Maffeo, S.J., *The Vatican Observatory in the Service of Nine Popes* (Vatican City: Vatican Observatory Publications, 2001), 5.

55. Details of the calculation can be found on the United States Naval Observatory (USNO) web page on the Date of Easter at *www.aa.usno.navy.mil/faq/docs/easter.html*.

the zodiac.[56] When the pope noticed that the spot of sunlight was far from its indicated position on March 21, he created a commission headed by a mathematician, Fr. Christopher Clavius, S.J. The calendar in use at that time was the Julian Calendar, which had a leap year every four years. Since the year is actually 365.2422 days long,[57] not quite 365.25, the approximation of the Julian Calendar, the leap years were adding too many days, approximately one full day every 128 years as these $0.25 - 0.2422 = 0.0078$ extra pieces of a day collected every year. By the time Gregory XIII noticed it, there were ten extra days between March 21 and the astronomical Vernal Equinox. To correct this, October 15, 1582, followed October 4 in Italy. In England and its colonies, September 14, 1752, followed Wednesday, September 2. The continuing correction is that century years that are not divisible by 400, such as 1700, are not leap years. Hence the English, who held to the Julian Calendar through 1700, taking it as a leap year, which the Gregorian calendar did not, had to subtract one day more than the Italians when they finally changed to the new calendar. For those of us in the United States, this calendar change caused confusion in the birthday of George Washington. He was born on February 11, 1732, under the Julian Calendar. Changing to the Gregorian Calendar and counting backward changed his birthday to February 22.

After the calendar change, the Vatican Observatory had a variety of incarnations, often struggling for recognition and funding from the church and pope. It was formally dedicated as *Specola Vaticana* (the Vatican mirror) in 1891 by Pope Leo XIII. This pope was also the first to issue an encyclical on social justice, *Rerum Novarum* (On the Condition of Workers), also in 1891.

Primarily, I learned astronomy at the Vatican Observatory as I participated in a project observing and classifying stars within 150

56. Maffeo, *The Vatican Observatory in the Service of Nine Popes,* 4.

57. This is an approximation, the length of the solar day (as opposed to the clock day), the month, and the year are far more complicated to define than is pertinent to this discussion. The curious reader is referred to a wealth of information on the Internet and the USNO's annual publication, *The Astronomical Almanac.*

light years of Earth with surface temperatures greater than about 3000K. I delighted in the much more hands-on activity of optical observing where the astronomers actually got to place the diffraction grating in the spectrograph and made various adjustments to the instrument. Of course, the actual "driving" of the telescope is kept in the competent hands of night assistants who know the telescope better than any astronomer visiting for a few nights a year possibly could, but there was still much more for the astronomers to do during optical observing than in radio. At the VLA, the astronomer's role in observing is limited to creating a file listing the sequence of sources to be observed. The telescope operators then execute the file and release the data to the astronomer at the end. The involvement with the actual workings of the telescope in optical astronomy engaged my love of the machines of astronomy, and I thrilled to the roars, whirrs, and clicks of the telescope as it opened to the stars, gathering photons that would tell us of their temperatures and sizes.

Though the work I did was confined to telescopes on Kitt Peak in Arizona and Cerro Tololo in Chile, the Vatican Observatory owns its own telescope on Mt. Graham in southeastern Arizona. The Vatican Advanced Technology Telescope, the VATT, is built around one of the first spin-cast mirrors made at the University of Arizona. Though it's often called the Pope Scope, the Vatican did not fund the telescope. Instead, the astronomers created the Vatican Observatory Foundation to raise the funds to build and maintain the VATT, which has now been in operation for over a decade.

Though I actually had very few discussions about faith and religion with the astronomers of the Vatican Observatory, living among people comfortable in both worlds strengthened my confidence in my own journey of faith and science. The University of Arizona Newman Center is across the street from Steward Observatory, which houses the offices of the Vatican Observatory. The 12:05 weekday Mass at the Newman Center fit easily into my schedule and attending it became my habit. Early on in my year there, the astronomer I worked most closely with, Chris Corbally, S.J., surprised me by showing up at Mass as the celebrant. Having Mass said by an astronomer, a man whose mind and knowledge I admired, nearly brought me to tears as my long-held sense of a fraud in two worlds crumbled in the face of the fact that I was not alone in my two-worldedness.

This is the greatest value in my continuing association with the Vatican Observatory: it gives me a community of Catholic astronomers who accept me into their midst. I did find them better able to compartmentalize their faith and religion than I have been. When I asked one how the universe changed when he spoke the words of consecration as priest, he responded that the spiritual and physical were in different realms, an answer I can't accept. I keep puzzling about how they might be knit together in the various Venn diagrams of chapter 10. The reason for this, I believe, is that all these men were educated by Jesuits and knew of scientists who were priests from their earliest school days.[58] This kept them from having to work through the sense of fraudulence I struggled with for years. My need to seek integrity in both science and faith prevented me from simply assigning them to different realms. I am one, integrated person who is both physical and spiritual and believe that the physical and spiritual universes are also integrated. Though I don't understand how they are integrated, I reject the idea of two realms and will continue to ask how spiritual acts change the physical universe. And my friends at the Vatican Observatory will support me in asking those questions and provide me a community where I can bring the data of my spiritual experiences to other scientists who share the journey.

---

58. When I finally connected with the Vatican Observatory, I felt as though I had bushwhacked alone up the trail-less mountain of putting science and religion together only to discover a bunch of guys who had simply driven to the top in a company car!

Chapter 14

Models of the Church

I N THE SAME DAY I can go from longing for monastic life to thinking
that I can't associate myself with Catholicism one minute longer.
Both of these reactions arise from my background as one who left
what I saw (and had experienced) as an uncaring, irrelevant institution having little to do with God, and one who knelt in humble
need in a New Mexico church and felt the touch of God's love in
the priest, the nuns, the people of the parish, and the sacraments of
Eucharist and Reconciliation. So the Aileen that fled and the Aileen
that returned stand together in the church trying to make sense of
it. It's not easy, but it is interesting, and it is the center of my life.

In a portion of the two-year Formation for Ministry[59] course in the
Diocese of Ogdensburg, I was assigned to read and write a paper on
Models of the Church by Avery Dulles.[60] I reflected on two of Dulles's
models of the church: the church as Institution and the church as
Servant. They seem to represent the aspects of the church, or perhaps
my images of the church, that caused me to flee, and touched me
with God's love when I returned.

As an academic I count among my peers mostly atheists (sometimes anti-theists) and almost all non-churchgoers. Many of them
are former Catholics, and though they accept my religious faith and
involvement as a part of me and do so with sometimes extraordinary generosity of spirit, religion is generally seen as a force for evil
in the world and the church as an archaic, obsolete institution that

---

59. This program continues in the diocese and enriches the lives of many lay Catholics.
60. Avery Dulles, *Models of the Church* (New York: Doubleday, Image Books, 1991).

would serve the world best by decaying to dust. They do not judge the philosophy of Jesus, or the ideals of the church this way, just the structures and history of the church, which is seen as having little, if anything, to do with Jesus and a lot to do with power as evidenced by the Crusades, the Spanish Inquisition, and silence in the face of the Holocaust. At least this is how I think they see it from having participated in many discussions both as a non-Catholic and as a "closet" Catholic.

I admit my membership in the church slowly in academic circles. By other academics, men and women, I get asked how I can associate myself with such an overtly and stubbornly sexist, hierarchical institution. In such situations, I can feel like my membership in the church is an act of treason against the fight for the equality of women. Yet I can almost at the same time feel that my mere speaking out for the full inclusion of women is an act of treason against the church that I, in many ways, deeply love.

So I struggle. When I joined the church as a graduate student, I did so out of a deep need for hope and faith in a God. In college I lost my need for a God to create the universe. This had been my childhood justification for faith; hence I lost my belief in God. I did retain both a suspicion and a hope that God did exist and did love me, but looked on these as unshakable remnants of childhood indoctrination, ignored them, and tried to banish them. I based my decisions and actions on a belief that there was no God. This belief did not, as many believers might suspect, make my world cold or empty. My world of graduate studies in physics and astronomy was a logical, orderly world filled with exploration of the wonders of the universe. It was also filled with challenge and warm, respectful human interactions even when they were competitive. Many people I know lead happy, fulfilling lives without any belief in God. But I couldn't do it. I despaired and struggled against depression and alcohol. It seemed I found life meaningless even as my life blossomed with possibilities, opportunities, and accomplishments. My view of the church began to change when I found Andrew Greeley's book *The Cardinal Sins* full of characters that were deep and kind and thoughtful — and found meaning in their practice of faith.[61] So, to my utter surprise (a surprise which lingers), I went to Mass at San Miguel parish and found myself immersed in a profound sense of meaning and connection with something beyond my humanity. I call it God, and I seek it in church, in the night sky, in my students puzzling about what Newton's laws have to do with the rest of their lives, and in myself as I struggle to imitate Jesus. But my atheism has not disappeared. Though I choose to practice belief that there is a God, I recognize that it is entirely possible that there is no God. Hence I practice my faith fully aware that all of it might be wrong and that parts of it are most likely wrong. So my faith is based on hope, not belief. I practice my faith in full light of the possibility that it's wrong because it helps me live better. Believing in a God of love who loves us, is aware of us, and invites us to deeper spiritual communion makes me a happier, kinder, more generous, less fearful, and less defensive human. It helps me to love and embrace life in spite of all its fears and griefs. So my view of the church is very different from that of someone who has always been in the church and does not so deeply question the most fundamental of the church's beliefs.

The model of the church that I identify most strongly as my own is that of servant. Dulles asserts that the development of the servant model arose from (or with) modernism: "The world has become increasingly active and independent of the church. The various sciences and disciplines have one by one emancipated themselves from church control, and . . . the world, generally speaking, feels justified in paying no heed [to the admonitions of the church]."[62] Since I live and work immersed in this modernism, it is entirely fitting that this model of the church resonates with me more than the other models where "the church is produced by God's direct action, and stands as a kind of mediator between God and the world." In reflecting on

---

61. Andrew Greeley, *The Cardinal Sins* (New York: Warner Books, 1982)
62. Dulles, *Models of the Church.*

this, I realize that I see the church as having an opportunity (and responsibility) to bring the message of Jesus to the world, but I do not see it as the only way that Jesus' message will be brought to the world. I do not doubt that if the church disappeared from Earth tomorrow, that God would still manage to teach humanity what Jesus taught. It made me very happy to find this view expressed in the Dogmatic Constitution on the Church, where the opening sentence says: "Christ is the light of humanity; and it is, accordingly, the heartfelt desire of this sacred Council . . . that, by proclaiming his Gospel to every creature, it may bring to all people that light of Christ which shines out visibly from the church" (no. 1). A later paragraph states that "many elements of sanctification and of truth are found outside its visible confines." But I still find myself somewhat uncomfortable with even the Vatican II documents because I don't believe that the church is here to "save" humanity.

God will "save" humanity (if it needs to be saved), but I don't think we need to be saved so much as taught. This shows my inclination for creation spirituality as opposed to redemption spirituality. I see the "fall" and "redemption" of humanity as metaphors for why we are so blind to God's love and what Christ came to teach us. I believe that the ultimate goal of life is for every person to fully realize the love of God for themselves, for other people, and for all of creation. Hence, the role of the church is to seek, experience, and cherish the love of God and, having touched and been transformed by it, to imitate it, proclaim it, teach of it, and invite everyone to recognize it and share in it. All of Dulles's models of the church do some of this, but it seems to me that the best way to teach is by example, and the example the church has been given is Jesus. I see Jesus as an example of someone whose awareness of God's love so filled him that not only could he continuously give of that love to humanity without being depleted, but he was compelled by its very presence to give of it. So he served humanity as a continuous act of love, accepting hate without returning hate. As Richard Rohr puts it, Jesus refused to crucify back even at the cost of being crucified.[63] This is the example I, as a Christian, am called to follow. And if I were Jesus, I suppose I could do it by myself, but I am not Jesus. So it takes the community, the church, to serve when (and where and in ways) I cannot serve and to support me so that I can grow toward a closer imitation of Christ. The action of God in the church (the "mystical" part of the communion) makes the whole of the church greater than the sum of its parts so that the world is served better by the church than it would be by the collection of individual church members. At the same time, the individuals in the church are also supported by it. Alone, I cannot sustain my awareness of God and God's love enough to imitate Jesus very closely at all, so I need the church to help me. I need its mystical communion: the community expressing God's love when I cannot touch it. I need its sacraments manifesting the presence of the holy when I cannot find it. I need its voice reminding me of what Jesus taught. And I suppose I even need its institutions to make the whole thing function, extract the wisdom of the community from our individual experiences, and even to hold me to the standards of Jesus and the community with its rules.

The models of the church other than the servant are, to me, necessary to sustain the members of the church so that they can serve the world in imitation of Christ. In his analysis, Dulles points out that the beneficiary of the servant model is the world, but that the beneficiaries of the other models are primarily the members of the church. One thing I have learned in my interactions with people in church is how little I comprehend what others believe is the benefit of being a member of the church. Whereas I see the church as supporting my own search for and experience of God so that I can imitate Christ in the world, I get the idea that others see the church as providing a path to heaven. This lack of comprehension on my part started to become clear to me in a Formation Program class discussion about the Dogmatic Constitution on the Church when it

---

63. Richard Rohr, *Broken and Blessed: A Retreat with Richard Rohr,* Credence Cassettes.

was pointed out how big a change it was for the church to recognize the validity of the beliefs and ideas of other Christian churches, non-Christian churches, the un-churched, and atheists. I can't imagine thinking that they are not valid! God is so beyond our comprehension, how could people think that there is only one path to God? And how can people think that there's some kind of a contest for getting into heaven and that the reason for church involvement is to chalk up a good score instead of to be transformed and "live in the fire of [Christianity's] creative action."[64] (Not that I manage to be so transformed. Mostly I'm probably trying to chalk up a good score, but I don't think that's the real goal of it!) I see this expressed in people's desire for the popes and bishops to declare "blacks and whites" as the defining absolute rules for us to live by in order to please God.

It seems to me in my modernist, academic, American view, that Jesus came not to give us rules, but freedom. Even St. Augustine said, "Love and do as you will." Yet it seems that people want the church to take away this freedom. They seem to want to exchange freedom for a certainty about how to attain heaven in the next life, even if it reduces this life to misery — our "exile in the valley of tears" according to the Hail! Holy Queen. Yet this life is such a precious and magnificent gift! It took the universe billions of years, a few generations of stars, and an unknown spark (that may just be God) to make people. Galaxies are much easier to make! In my years of studying and teaching astronomy, I have found myself becoming more and more amazed by what surrounds us on Earth. I look at stars, clouds, dandelions, mosquitoes, and cows, and I am amazed. I look at myself looking, knowing I'm looking, and knowing I'm amazed, and I am overwhelmed with awe. What an incredible thing to be alive and to know that I am alive! To hear people reduce this magnificence to a "valley of tears" causes me deep anguish. People are the most wondrous things in the universe but they don't know it, even as

---

64. Teilhard de Chardin as cited in Blanche Gallagher, *Meditations with Teilhard de Chardin* (Santa Fe: Bear & Co., 1988).

they walk around immersed in the beauty of Earth and sky. Thomas Merton saw the wonder of people at the corner of Fourth and Walnut in Louisville, Kentucky. "I was suddenly overwhelmed with the realization that I loved all those people, that they were mine and I theirs, that we could not be alien to one another even though we were total strangers. . . . And if only everybody could realize this! But it cannot be explained. There is no way of telling people that they are all walking around shining like the sun."[65] Jesus said that the Kingdom of God is in our midst, and I believe that all we need to do to attain it is to realize that we are already there. A Zen-Catholic view, perhaps, but it leaves me struggling to comprehend how people accept and teach their children that they are essentially displeasing to God (original sin), that life is a trial, a test to be passed in order to become pleasing enough to God and get to heaven, and that religion is about how to pass that test. I don't hear this in the words of Jesus and find myself blaming the institutionalized church (as Dulles identifies it) for propagating it.

Fyodor Dostoyevsky personified the institutionalized church as the Grand Inquisitor in the *Brothers Karamazov*.[66] The old cardinal of Seville, who has just burned one hundred heretics at the stake, finds Jesus on the steps of the cathedral and arrests him. In the prison the Inquisitor describes to Jesus how he erred when he resisted the temptations of the devil in the desert and chose to give humanity freedom instead of the "miracle, mystery, and authority" characterized by turning the stones to bread, jumping off a cliff to be caught by angels, and accepting political power. The Inquisitor claims that he and the institutional church are being kind to humanity by having the Inquisition because it takes away the burden of freedom from people. The Inquisitor says to Jesus:

---

65. Thomas Merton, *Conjectures of a Guilty Bystander* (New York: Doubleday, 1965), 156–57.

66. Fyodor Dostoyevsky, *The Brothers Karamazov* (New York: Vintage Books, 1991), 288–311.

You wanted man's free love so that he should follow you freely, fascinated and captivated by you. Instead of strict ancient law, man had in the future to decide for himself with a free heart what is good and what is evil, having only your image before him for guidance. But did it never occur to you that he would at last reject and call in question even your image and your truth, if he were weighed down by so fearful a burden as freedom of choice? They will at last cry aloud that the truth is not in you, for it was impossible to leave them in greater confusion and suffering than you have done by leaving them with so many cares and insoluble problems.

He claims that only a few scores of thousands will be able to accept their freedom (the "narrow gate") while thousands of millions will suffer misery because

> ...a free mind and science will lead them into such a jungle and bring them face to face with such marvels and insoluble mysteries that some of them, the recalcitrant and the fierce, will destroy themselves, others, recalcitrant but weak, will destroy one another, and the rest, weak and unhappy, will come crawling to our feet and cry aloud: "Yes, you were right, you alone possessed his mystery and we come back to you — save us from ourselves!"

This is what I hear when someone in the church states that knowledge is too dangerous for most people and that what we really need to study is basic Catholic doctrine. It is also what I hear from those who criticize all who do not live by their version of Catholicism and seem to gloat over their (real or imagined) struggles and failings. It is the voice of the Inquisitor that I hear in pronouncements that deny women the opportunity to follow whatever call we might think we hear from God, deny the community the freedom to openly discuss the issue, and deny God the freedom to call whomever God wants to be priests.

I even hear the echo of the Inquisitor's voice in the Dogmatic Constitution on the Church, where it states that the Roman Pontiff "has full supreme and universal power over the whole church, a power which he can always exercise unhindered" and that the bishops are "teachers endowed with the authority of Christ." How can any person or group of people be certain that they express the will of God? It seems to me that God usually proves to be much weirder than the pontiff and bishops and the rest of us expect. It also seems to me that Jesus did not admire hierarchical authority. I think the structures of the church are human (specifically Greek, Roman, and mediaeval European) inventions, not divine decrees. In these human structures proclaimed divine, the Inquisitor yet walks the corridors of our church, and the odor of burning flesh lingers in his willingness to destroy people for the sake of doctrinal loyalty. I see the very message and love of Christ that the Servant church should be busy delivering to humanity contradicted and made to appear as a mockery by the Inquisitor's attitude that "it is neither the free verdict of their hearts nor love that matters, but the mystery which they must obey blindly, even against their conscience." Richard Rohr identifies this attitude as institutionalized violence, which crushes individuals with phrases like "we've always done it this way."

I am frightened and offended by the Inquisitor, and my reaction is to flee from him. Hence when I glimpse him in the church, in parish meetings or pronouncements from Rome, a sense that this church is still his church sweeps over me. When this happens I become convinced that I was right when I fled this church and that all my sense of God's touch must just be the delusions of a mind unable to free itself from early indoctrination.

Faith, however tells me that this church is not the Inquisitor's church. It is God's church. The God who refused the devil's offers in the desert and chose to give humanity freedom promised that the gates of hell (personified by the Inquisitor) would not prevail against it. For the most part, the documents of Vatican II point to a church where the Inquisitor would not be welcome. So I stay. But though he won't prevail, I sense that the Inquisitor will not disappear. So how do I live with his presence?

My first response is to analyze why the Inquisitor remains. Why do people cling to rules? Why do I even find in myself a need and a desire for a church that demands obedience to what it truly knows to be right behavior (and attitudes) in the eyes of God? Looking within myself, I find that the need arises from my ignorance of God, and that the desire arises from my lack of confidence in being able to find my own way along the Godly path. I really do need the wisdom of the experience of others, and I am helped by being held accountable to the standards that I profess. I think that what may be the difference between me and the Inquisitor is that I do not fear God's condemnation. I seek God's love, or more knowledge and experience of God's love, and right behavior and attitudes are necessary to be able to accept that love, but I don't think that God condemns anybody — not even Hitler. Even though words in the Gospel about the judgment day are attributed to Jesus, the idea of it is too incongruous with the rest of his message about the love and forgiveness of God for me to accept the heaven/hell scenario that many people seem to accept. I think we can condemn ourselves by living so badly, so unlovingly, that when we do face God we cannot forgive ourselves enough to bear being in God's presence, but I don't think God condemns us. I get the idea that this isn't what most Catholics think and I suspect that the reason some cling so tightly to the institutionalized church and judge others' holiness by adherence to rules is that they do fear condemnation. My reaction to this idea is to think that a way for me to cope with the Inquisitor (even in myself) is to recognize that in trying to restrict the freedom of others, he is reducing his own freedom (by having to hold the other end of the rope he's tied them to) out of his need for the certainty of doctrine and either fear or incomprehension of God actually loving us and calling us to love as God loves. I understand this in the rare moments when I get a glimpse of what Jesus actually calls us to and must face how far I am from it. At those times I do fear that I won't be able to bear his presence and must admit to finding myself reaching to wrap adherence to church doctrine around me like a shawl to ward off the chill of the night.

My second response to the presence of the Inquisitor is to figure out how to respond to him. Since my religion is about imitating Christ, I guess I should look to him. Jesus faced the Inquisitor. And Jesus condemned the Inquisitor in the form of the Pharisees for judging and burdening people. Yet Jesus did not fight the Inquisitor; he submitted to him and forgave him. It seems like a perfectly clear answer: speak out against the Inquisitor and submit to the church, even when it's the Inquisitor's church. I was once told by a conservative Catholic woman to "offer up" my suffering over sexism as my cross and accept it. Is that what it would mean to imitate Christ? I think not, because Jesus didn't submit to all the rules: he talked to women, he performed miracles on the Sabbath, and he called himself the Son of God. But he did submit to crucifixion. Why? What's the difference? Did he submit to crucifixion because not submitting would have required him to either engage in violence if he used human means, or to deprive humanity of freedom if he used divine means, whereas not submitting to the Sabbath laws required neither of these? So what does submission mean to me? Mostly it seems to mean struggle. Part of me wants to submit wholly to the church. I know that I don't know very much about God (though I'll rarely admit it), and I do need others to teach me and lead me to God. The value of obedience is extolled by many spiritual writers because of how it tames the will and expresses faith in God and the structures and authorities God has provided. I want to practice and express such faith in God, and I think I do practice obedience in "listening intently" to what the church says, though not, necessarily, in complying with every decree. But, as the Inquisitor says, God has given me freedom to follow him by deciding with a free heart what is good and what is evil, and blind submission to the church seems a failure to take up my responsibility. The church has shown by its history that it is not always a force for good. Horrors have been perpetrated with the approval of the church. Thus, I can't believe that I am called by

God to support its every pronouncement and doctrine, particularly when I see them as contrary to the message of the gospel. The institutionalized sexism of the church is evil and destructive in the same way that racism is, and it contributes to the cultural acceptance of devaluation and abuse of women, children, and many men. It testifies that not all people image Christ equally and that a person's ability to image Christ can be judged by that person's outward appearance. In this case and others, I believe I'm called to serve the church by speaking out against what I see as evil so that the church, like all of us humans, can grow in holiness and closeness to God. The tough part is trying to figure out if I contribute to the perpetration of evil by participating in the church even if I do speak out against it. Sometimes it gets very tough to decide whether to stay or flee because in both choices I betray people I love and in both choices I seem to betray God. Such is the misery of God's gift of the freedom to decide good and evil with a free heart.

This dilemma has been with me for the twenty-five years I have been back in the church, and though I have sometimes fled for weeks or months, I have found myself more strongly called to stay than go. So I guess I will continue to speak out my convictions as I struggle to be humble enough to follow my call to be obedient to the church. And I will continue seeking to know the will of God and practicing the faith that God is at work in this church, even as God is at work in me, calling us both to serve, to love, and to forgive.

Chapter 15

Seeking the Light

YEARS AFTER finishing my Ph.D., I lay on the floor of the dome beneath the two-hundred-inch telescope at Palomar Observatory. A graduate student was observing the spectra of galaxies in Hercules. I could see the stars of Hercules, but the galaxies were too faint for me to see since nearly half a billion light years of space stretched between us. This particular cluster has many spiral galaxies like our own Milky Way. Two of them that we see face-on, near the center of the image on page 143, are colliding and share the single name of NGC 6050.[67] Many others of them are edge-on. The student was taking spectra of these edge-on spiral galaxies to determine the speeds of the stars orbiting the center of the galaxy. Our sun orbits the center of the Milky Way at over half a million miles per hour. Since it is the mass of the galaxy that determines the orbital speed of the stars, this student was "weighing" galaxies with her spectrograph.

Periodically, I would hear the motors kick on to move the huge, but delicate telescope to aim at a different galaxy. Sometimes this would be accompanied by clanking and roaring as the huge dome shifted so as not to block any of the faint light. Abruptly, all would fall silent when the telescope and dome took their positions. Moments later, a faint whirring would let me know that the shutter was open. As I lay there on the floor I knew I was bathed in galactic light half a billion years old, too faint for me to see. When that light left the galaxy, life flourished only in the oceans of Earth and had not yet ventured out

---

67. Most galaxies carry many names, some from a variety of catalogs. NGC here refers to the New General Catalog that was first published in 1888.

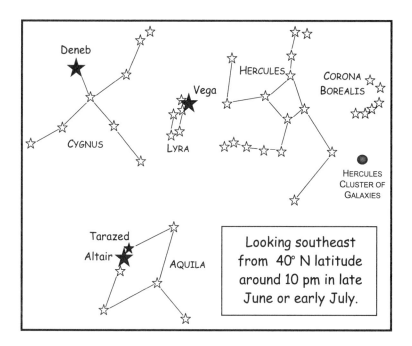

Deneb

HERCULES

CORONA
BOREALIS

Vega

CYGNUS

LYRA

HERCULES
CLUSTER OF
GALAXIES

Tarazed

Altair

AQUILA

Looking southeast
from 40° N latitude
around 10 pm in late
June or early July.

onto the land. North America straddled the equator and the rocks into which the skyscrapers of midtown and downtown Manhattan were being laid down as sediments in the Iapetus Ocean, a precursor of today's Atlantic. The rocks of Palomar Mountain on which the observatory dome rested would not rise from the Earth's interior until the light had traversed 75 percent of that distance. I thought of those ancient photons falling around and upon me like tiny, invisible hailstones. When I heard the click of the shutter closing, I knew that some of the photons had fallen into the telescope and diffracted off the grating to create the spectrum. I was awed to think that after half a billion years of travel, some of those photons had arrived at a place where a mind was looking for them and could decipher the information they carried about their home galaxy so very far away. My sense of awe brought me to tears and to prayer.

Spectroscopy

Other than a few moon rocks and meteorites, all we know of the universe beyond Earth we have learned from the electromagnetic waves that continually and gratuitously fall on our planet. Though people have gazed at the stars for millennia, it is only in the past few centuries that we have begun to discover the wealth of information knitted into the depth and breadth of the electromagnetic spectrum.

Since creatures first looked up to see the rainbow, we've been aware of the spectrum. Ancient people were also aware that clear crystals, such as those of quartz, produce rainbows in sunlight. But it was Newton, working with prisms in 1666, who realized that the colors were not from the crystal, but components of the light itself. In 1814, the telescope maker Joseph von Fraunhofer observed dark lines (still referred to as Fraunhofer lines) in the spectra of stars and noted different sets of lines in different stars. He went on to make the first diffraction grating that produces a spectrum by reflection, avoiding the losses of intensity and quality from the light's passing through a prism. If you've noticed the rainbow from light reflected off a CD, you've seen a diffraction grating. In 1826, John Herschel and W. H. Fox Talbot discovered that heated gases produce spectra of bright lines that are characteristic of the elements present. Thus we realized that the dark lines in the spectrum of the stars revealed the elements present. In laboratories worldwide, work commenced on determining the sets of lines belonging to elements and molecules. At the same time, physicists began puzzling about the properties and structure of atoms and molecules that could give rise to these lines.

Neils Bohr first described the source of the bright and dark lines in spectra. In 1911, Ernest Rutherford, working with Hans Geiger (of "Geiger counter" fame), had determined that the atom consisted of a tiny nucleus surrounded by a cloud of "orbiting" electrons. Rutherford is also famous for stating, "In science there is only physics; everything else is stamp collecting" — which physicists love to quote to colleagues in biology, geology, and, not unimportantly, astronomy!

Hercules Cluster of Galaxies.
Photo courtesy of NOAO/AURA/NSF

Rutherford's early model of the atom, with the electrons orbiting the nucleus, was Bohr's starting point. He determined that the electrons could not be in just any orbit, but only orbits with specific energies, determined by the interaction of the electrons and nucleus.

Electrons can change orbit only by absorbing or emitting a photon, a particle of light, a bundle of energy. The energy of the light must equal the difference in the energy of the levels between which the electron is moving. A poor analogy is that one must eat a hotdog, the human equivalent of absorbing a photon, to climb to a higher row of seats in a stadium. Of course, the analogy breaks down since it's not necessary to give up the hotdog to back down but it is necessary to go back down to give up the hotdog! Another way this analogy breaks down is that the electron doesn't "move" as we think of moving. It can't exist between the energy levels, called states. It simply stops existing at one state as it simultaneously begins existing in the other state. This is the true definition of a quantum leap. Even Captain Kirk's "Beam me up, Scotty" was not a quantum leap as the transporter physically moved the captain's energy signature between locations, though the transportee was not aware of this motion and felt as though he had, indeed, made a quantum leap. Except Doctor McCoy, of course, who seemed to have suffered every nanosecond of the entire process.

Traveling home on the California Zephyr train from CMC after learning of Bohr's model of the atom and the process of light, I watched sparks rising from the wheels and track and struggled to wrap my mind around the idea that the light of those sparks was due to electrons cascading down to lower energy levels. I was mesmerized.

Stellar Spectra and the Vatican Observatory

While the physicists were working to explain the spectral lines, astronomers were busy observing, cataloging, and classifying the spectra of stars. In 1850, Fr. Angelo Secchi, S.J., was named the director of the Vatican Observatory.[68] An energetic astronomer and administrator, he had an observatory built on the roof of the Church of St. Ignatius in Rome to house the twenty-four-inch telescope he acquired through use of his assistant's inheritance. He used a round prism to observe more than four thousand stars and classify them by their spectra, developing four classes.[69] For this, he is known as the father of stellar spectroscopy, but as with all fathering, after the initial act, the bulk of the work was done by women.

Williamina Paton Fleming was hired as a maid by Edward Pickering, the director of the Harvard College Observatory, after her husband abandoned her and her unborn son shortly after their immigrating to Boston from Scotland. Pickering faced thousands of photographic plates being obtained by the observatory needing to

---

68. Sabino Maffeo, S.J., *The Vatican Observatory in the Service of Nine Popes* (Vatican City: Vatican Observatory Publications, 2001), 14.

69. Ibid., 16.

be analyzed. According to the *Women Working* collection at Harvard University,[70] Pickering became frustrated by the poor work of his male employees and "reportedly declared that his maid could do a better job."[71] In 1881, Fleming began to work at the observatory and was to transform stellar spectroscopy. She found Secchi's classification system too crude, and created a new system based on the absorption lines of hydrogen, cataloging stars from A through N. Fleming was the first American woman elected to the Royal Astronomical Society (in 1906) and presided over other women working at the observatory, known as the "Harvard Computers" since they did many tedious computations. I love sharing with my students that the first computers were rooms full of women! They were also known as "Pickering's Harem" or "Pickering's Women" and did much to advance our understanding of the universe. Antonia Maury, an 1887 Vassar graduate, further refined the classification system, placing the lettered categories in order of temperature: O B A F G K M. For generations, the mnemonic used for this order has been "Oh, be a fine girl, kiss me," not the mnemonic one would expect for a classification scheme created primarily by women, though most of us simply changed girl to guy.[72] Annie Jump Cannon, who said of the spectra, "They aren't just streaks to me; each new spectrum is the gateway to a wonderful new world. It is almost as if the distant stars had really acquired speech and were able to tell of their constitution and physical condition."[73] Cannon classified almost half a million stars in her lifetime and some of the stars I have classified, were last classified by her. Cecila Payne Gaposchkin was the first to earn a Ph.D. for work at the Harvard

---

70. Harvard University Open Collections Program, *Women Working, 1800–1930* (*www.ocp.hul.harvard.edu/ww/index.html*).

71. Harvard University Library Open Collections Program: Williamina Paton Stevens Fleming (*ocp.hul.harvard.edu/ww/people_fleming.html*).

72. My colleague and I have mnemonic contests for our astronomy students every semester, and so far the best mnemonic is "Observing Betelgeuse at four am? Gee, Kill Me."

73. Jennifer H. Powell, "A Century Ago, Women Astronomers at Harvard Made Scientific History," *Harvard University Gazette*, March 19, 1998 (*www.hno.harvard.edu/gazette/1998/03.19/ReachingfortheS.html*).

College Observatory by determining the actual temperatures of the gases that would give rise to the different spectra. Due to the work of these women, we are able to determine not only the elements present in the stars, but their temperatures. Other work in spectroscopy has also enabled us to determine more details about the stars from the spectra, such as their sizes and rotation rates.

Motion toward or away from the observer is easily determined from spectra. Christian Doppler had realized that the change in tone of a passing sound — the roar of a NASCAR engine, a siren, or a train whistle — was due to the motion's effect of squashing or stretching the sound waves as it approached or receded from the observer. In the second half of the nineteenth century, Armand Fizeau was able to show this also applied to light as well, with the approaching source's "higher tone" being bluer and the receding source's "lower tone" being redder. These shifts in the color, along with the fact that we know the wavelengths of spectral lines to very high precision (e.g., the wavelength of the hydrogen line that colors photographs of nebulae red is 656.281 nanometers, that is, 0.656281 micrometers, or a bit more than half a thousandth of a millimeter) allows us to determine the motion of anything producing spectral lines, that is, any star or galaxy or cloud of gas. For instance, from its blue shift, we know that the star Vega is approaching us at a speed of 14 km/s, whereas the red shift of Caph shows it is receding at 11 km/s.

The startling and disconcerting discovery that the universe is expanding came from Edwin Hubble's observations and measurements of the red shifts of galaxies. He took many long-exposure photographs of "spiral nebulae," seeking to determine if they were objects within our Milky Way galaxy or other galaxies. At the Harvard College Observatory, one of Pickering's women, Henrietta Leavitt, had studied variable stars like Delta Cephei, visible most of the year in northern skies over North America, Europe, and Asia. She compared the period over which they vary to their inherent brightness, their luminosity, and found them to be proportional. Bright stars vary more slowly than dim stars. This meant that observing the period of

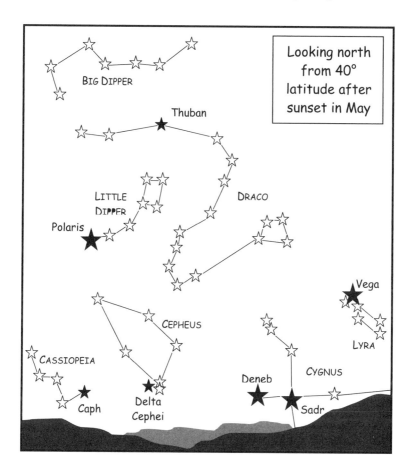

Looking north
from 40°
latitude after
sunset in May

BIG DIPPER

Thuban

LITTLE
DIPPER

DRACO

Polaris

Vega

CEPHEUS

LYRA

CASSIOPEIA

CYGNUS

Deneb

Caph

Delta
Cephei

Sadr

variation of a "Cepheid Variable" could give a measure of its luminosity. How bright it is in our sky, its "apparent magnitude," is easily
measured on photographic plates or electronic detectors. The difference in the apparent and absolute magnitudes is determined by the
distance to the star.[74] By taking multiple photographs of each spiral
nebula, Hubble was able to identify Cepheid Variables and determine

---

74. The relationship is that the apparent magnitude or luminosity, L, is related to the
apparent magnitude or flux, F by the square of the distance d: $L = (4\pi d^2) F$.

their periods of variation. This and the apparent magnitude determined from the photographs gave him a measure of the distances to these objects. He discovered they were much farther away than any objects in our own galaxy, and by that, must be galaxies themselves. Obtaining red shifts of the galaxies, Hubble compared them to the distances and discovered that all but a very few close galaxies are moving away from us and the more distant galaxies are moving away faster. These are the data on which the Big Bang theory is based.

As I lay on the floor of Palomar Observatory, underneath the very telescope in which Edwin Hubble spent many nights, the photons detected by the telescope revealed the speed of the stars and nebulae they had left in their red and blue shifts. From these, the speeds of those billions of stars, the rotation speed of the galaxy was determined. Through physics, the physics Newton developed in the seventeenth century, the mass required for the stars and nebulae to orbit the center of the galaxy at those speeds was simple to calculate. In fact, the student had been working with the spectra long enough to be able to estimate the mass of the galaxy as soon as she saw the spectrum. From where I lay, however, knowing I could not see the details revealed by the telescope, I also sensed a spiritual realm that I also could not see, and wondered about its details.

The Light of the World

Associating God with light is one of the most ancient of our ideas about God. Throughout much of human history, the sun, our local star, has been worshiped as God. Knowing what we now know about light, what does this metaphor tell us about God?

The history of astronomy is mostly a tale of how we learned to see the light. We learned to use prisms and diffraction gratings to reveal hidden details of chemical composition and motion. We learned to make telescopes that detect cosmic radiation in nonvisible bands of the spectrum from radio to gamma rays. We have learned how to extract information about the universe that has been there all along, but beyond our unaided senses to detect. For all we've learned, though, light remains incomprehensible with its wave-particle duality.

If God is light, what are the qualities of God that we must learn to detect? Looking at the variety of religions, I wonder if different cultures might be attuned to different aspects of God just as radio and infrared telescopes are attuned to different aspects of the electromagnetic spectrum. Just as we observe the universe in all wavelengths so as to know the fullness of its processes, is it possible that seeking God in all the traditions of humankind could help us to know the fullness of God? The Buddhists are most attuned to the "otherness" of God, the Hindus the variability of God, the Jews, the actions of God in the world, the Muslims, the majesty of God, the Christians, the approachability of God, and the Earth religions the ubiquity of God. Perhaps someday we will all recognize that we are all viewing the same God through different lenses, none of which is opaque, but none of which reveals the entirety of God.

Within each religion, the differences in sects and habits — Orthodox and Reformed, Sunni and Shi'te, Catholic and Protestant — may be the spectral lines. Even within a single church there are spectral lines: Jesuit vs. Benedictine, Mother Angelica Followers vs. Call to Action members, restorationists vs. progressives. It is most natural and easiest to believe that only our point of view, only our own spiritual spectral line is the truth about God and those other people are all nuts. But perhaps they are just showing us a different aspect of God and the best way to learn of the fullness of God is to listen to their point of view. Not that I'm at all good at this, but I do recognize its value as I recognize that it takes all colors to make white light and all the spectral bands to teach us of the universe.

Chapter 16

The Practice of Faith

ORE THAN A DECADE after I joined the church, I met someone who would journey with me for nearly ten years of the ups and downs of life and for thirty days of silence with the Spiritual Exercises of St. Ignatius. Tom Clarke, S.J., was one of my dearest friends and knew me better than any other human, including my mom. In one of our many talks in person, over the phone, or via email, Tom gave me a definition of faith that I have recited many times in many venues. According to Tom, faith is

1. a gift
2. a decision, and
3. not contrary to reason.

This definition has guided my thinking and my spiritual journey and deepened my understanding of my own experiences with God and with the church.

Faith Is a Gift

I was driven to faith by my experiences of contact with a "who" beyond myself. These experiences were gifts in that they were unbidden and that they did not demand any return. I ultimately desired to respond to them, but they were not given on that condition. There were other gifts, though, that gave me faith. QB's appearance in my dorm room and companionship through sixteen difficult years was certainly a gift. Her delight in life and in my presence were immense gifts that coaxed me through some very dark days. The scriptures and other writings on faith, God, and religious traditions are also gifts helping us to know that we are not the first or the only people to struggle with faith. Religious rituals, too, can be gifts that help us through times when it's very hard to believe. Like making your face smile to lighten your mood, the physical action can sometimes lead the mind. There are also uncountable little gifts contributing to my faith that give me solace, hope, and perseverance when I have needed it most.

If faith is a gift, though, and God is loving and generous, why doesn't everyone have faith? Is it not given to them? I wonder if my sense of the whoness is, in fact, some kind of a sense akin to the five senses we know people have. My colleagues in science are revolted by the idea, but I'm not willing to say that it's impossible. We just know too little about our own brains to reject it outright. If it is a sense, perhaps some people don't have it, just as some are blind or deaf. Or perhaps they have it and interpret the experiences differently. That's very possible. Some will say that my early experiences of religion imprinted the interpretation of God onto experiences of a normal meditative state. If I hadn't been told these experiences were contact with God, I wouldn't interpret them that way. That very well may be true. But why do some people raised as atheists come to faith and others raised in churches reject it? Do we all have the same experiences? It's impossible to know. I believe that God does call to each of us in ways we are capable of hearing — or detecting somehow. But God is always elusive. Though I believe God is shouting at us of the wonder and love of the universe, I think that shouting is so knitted into the ordinary and the normal it's as hard to detect as the dark against the night.

Faith Is a Decision

Many people express surprise when I tell them how deliberately I choose faith. Initially, it was a decision to accept my experience of a relationship with nature, with the whoness as a relationship with God. That decision required me to recognize the ambiguity of arguments for and against the existence of God, the weirdness of the universe that may just be enough for God to exist, and the weirdness of my self-conscious, self-reflective self much weirder than anything the laws of physics, chemistry, and biology could presently predict. Choosing faith, however, was not a mystical once-and-for-all decision. My inner atheist is still very much alive because there is no objective, reproducible evidence for the existence of God, and I have no guarantee that my experiences of relationship with God are not delusion or the imprint of Catholic indoctrination on a natural meditative state. Thus I have to remake my decision to practice faith every day and am both puzzled and a bit envious of those who cite the moment they "accepted Christ as my personal savior" with the same completeness and finality as citing the day their appendix was removed. As though atheism can't grow back any more than an appendix can.

In face of my profound doubt in the existence of God, I am forced to examine why I choose to practice faith. Ultimately, it's because I am a happier, more confident person capable of making a greater contribution to humanity and the universe as a person of faith than I could be as an atheist. This is not quite Pascal's wager about the afterlife where if God does not exist it doesn't matter if one is religious but if the church is right, being an atheist could have terrible consequences. Instead, it's a pragmatic choice to "go with my gut feeling" that God does exist in the face of contradictory and, ultimately, insufficient, data.

To continue making this decision in the face of the very contrary data of the world's violence and unfairness in the face of great wealth and prosperity takes deliberate effort. For me it takes continuous, frequent contact with other believers, which is my reason for belonging to a church. But since most of the churchgoers I know don't frequently talk about their atheism, if it is present, I also need to read of others who struggle with their beliefs. Karen Armstrong and Kathleen Norris have been extremely helpful authors for me. Beyond these, I also need to seek other intellectuals and scientists who ask similar questions about the entire idea of God and the workings of the universe. This led me to the Sisters of St. Joseph of Concordia, Tom Clarke, and the Vatican Observatory. Lastly, I need to spend time within myself exploring the relationship that first led me to faith, which led me to morning Mass, to chanting with the monks of the Monastery of Christ in the Desert, striving to practice the mindfulness of Thich Nhat Hanh, and times of prayer in my own living room, petting my animals and watching the birds at my feeder.

Deciding to continue practicing faith with the Roman Catholic Church requires me to seek out similarly minded Catholics, which I manage mostly through subscribing to intellectual and somewhat liberal publications such as *America, Commonweal, The National Catholic Reporter,* and *Conscience.* I also subscribe to *Sojourners* and *Ode* magazines, which are supportive of the liberal Christian and just plain liberal striving toward personal and societal compassion. But staying with the church requires more; it requires being open to the possibility that things I am hard-pressed to believe may be true, or at least true in ways very different from our everyday experience — which leads naturally to the third element in Tom's definition of faith.

Faith Is Not Contrary to Reason

I would guess that very few people would include this notion in the definition of faith. In fact, I imagine that most people assume the exact opposite; that one must believe in the unreasonable and impossible to believe in God. It is assumed that to be Catholic one must believe that Jesus was born to a virgin, that he turned two fish and five loaves into enough to feed thousands, that he physically rose from the dead with the ability to appear, disappear, walk through walls, and eat fish. It is assumed that one must believe that God can and does suspend physical laws to split the Red Sea, lead the Hebrews through the desert, and lead the Magi to Bethlehem with a star.

As an astronomer, a physicist, a scientist, I am hard pressed to believe the miraculous events in scripture and tradition as actual, physical events. Most of them, I assume, are metaphors trying to express a spiritual, not a historical, truth. The idea that ancient writers, as well as translators through the centuries "channeled God" with 100 percent accuracy is quite difficult for anyone who has known actual people. If someone today claimed to be writing the actual word of God, we'd likely suggest psychological therapy. And if a council added or excluded books from scripture there would be widespread accusations of political manipulation no matter which books they were. Perhaps others can believe that people in the past were less susceptible to the assumptions of their own culture, the desires of their own egos, or the temptations of power, but I figure that people haven't changed significantly in millennia. Evolution is slow and the difference between us and those who first put stylus to clay or pen to parchment is at best, minuscule. So I read scripture much as I read a modern book about spirituality: as people's struggle to express and try to make sense of this God thing with the lingual and cultural tools at hand.

For example, the Epic of Gilgamesh, which dates from about two thousand years before Jesus was born in Bethlehem, says this:

> Child of Lugalbanda's wife and some great force,
> Gilgamesh is a fate alive, the
> finest babe of Ninsun, she who never
> let a man touch her, indeed
> so pure and heavenly, so without sin.[75]

This made me realized that a virgin birth might simply be a common way for ancient writers to express the uniqueness of a person. If someone had such a unique origin, that person must be a unique and holy individual. I don't see it as profoundly different from the

---

75. Danny P. Jackson, *The Epic of Gilgamesh* (Wauconda, IL: Bolchazy-Carducci Publishers, 1992), Tablet 1, 2

current "born with a silver spoon" metaphor that we use to express a birth into wealth. The metaphorical, allegorical interpretation of scripture does not mean that there is no truth in scripture; it means that the truth is not literal, but deeper, more subtle and spiritual. For me to stay in the church, when I hear the stories from scripture, often interpreted literally by homilists, I need to work past my unbelief to seek a spiritual truth independent of the physical or historical accuracy of the account.

The resurrection of Jesus is a scriptural account for which this has taken great effort. I don't know the physics or biology of what happened to Jesus, but I would not be surprised or disturbed if his desiccated body were discovered in a cave in Qumran.[76] What I have come to believe about the resurrection is that the transformation of the Apostles was an extraordinary event perhaps only expressible through the language of resurrection. Here were a bunch of scared guys hiding in a shuttered room who had an experience so profound that they not only left hiding, but boldly proclaimed the very thing they thought would get them killed, and in the end, did get them killed! What happened to transform them so dramatically? Scripture tells us they named their experience an encounter with the Risen Christ. What, exactly, that means in the physical universe is not something we can know scientifically from the information at hand. In astronomy there are many things we don't know — what started the Big Bang? — so I am not uncomfortable saying that I don't know what the resurrection of Jesus means. What matters is that it was transformative for the Apostles. In my spiritual journey, I seek such transformative experiences. I've had some, though none with the profound result of that of the Apostles. In this book, I've tried to express those experiences and know that my words fail to convey their reality. When I read of the Apostles' description of the Risen Christ, I realize they are trying to convey an experience far beyond the ability of words to describe. I strive to refrain from puzzling about

---

76. The area in the West Bank where the Dead Sea Scrolls were discovered in 1947.

what cameras and meters would have detected and "rest in unknowing," seeking my own "experience of the Living Christ," whatever that may be.

In fact, I actively strive to interpret descriptions of supernatural events in scripture as metaphor. For instance, the "feeding of the five thousand" with five loaves and two fish (Matt. 14:14–21), I take not as a miracle of creating fish and bread out of nothing, but a miracle of getting everyone there to share what they had. At the end of the story, the Gospel of Matthew says "those who ate were about five thousand men, not counting women and children." Well, they may not have counted, but I can't imagine women with children following their men out into the wilderness without packing supplies. The men might have neglected this, but it's a rare mother who isn't prepared with something to feed the kids. However, none of them knew if others had brought food and were concerned that if they brought theirs out, they would not have enough for themselves and to share with those around them. So they kept their supplies to themselves. When Jesus and the disciples started sharing their meager loaves and fishes, though, it encouraged others to share what they had and, lo and behold, everyone ate. Since the point of the spiritual journey is to change people's attitudes, particularly their generosity with each other, this explanation seems much more fitting to the gospel message than a miraculous invention of bread and fish.

My seeking to interpret supernatural miracles as metaphor is motivated by a number of things. First, I know of no objective evidence for any miracles as the suspension of physical law. Miracles very well may occur, but it would take solid, irrefutable evidence to convince me that the laws of physics, chemistry, or biology were actually suspended. This is because such extremely weird and even miraculous things can occur in complete accord with physical law. In my astronomy class last year, a student stepped into the hallway during a break to have a chat with a friend in Nepal! He was talking to the other side of the world from the corridor outside my lab. As I have been writing this book, I've been keeping the files on two computers and a flash drive an inch long and half-inch wide. I can store this entire book on a stick smaller than a pack of gum! If these miracles can occur within physical law, I see no need to suspend it. What we actually observe across the universe seems much more "miraculous" than any of the miracle stories in scripture!

Faith based on miraculous events is subject to damage or loss if those events are somehow shown to have not occurred as reported. As I write this, a book by Simcha Jacobovici and Charles Pellegrino is reporting the finding of the tombs of Jesus and his family in Jerusalem.[77] If by some means it can be proven that the ossuary marked "Jesus, Son of Joseph" does contain the bones of Jesus, some Christians with faith based on Jesus being physically subsumed into heaven after his resurrection could have their faith deeply shaken and even destroyed. Having been through a loss of faith when I no longer needed God to create the universe, I know what a difficult journey it can be. Thus my faith is based on my own experiences of God vetted, as well as they can be, with the experiences of others on the spiritual journey. Some will say I'm not actually a Christian if I don't believe scripture as literal historical truth, don't believe that Jesus was conceived without sex,[78] or that he physically rose from the dead. But that's ok. I'm not a Christian to satisfy anyone else's definition, I am a Christian primarily because it's what I grew up with and am familiar with, but also because the teachings of Jesus resonate with my experiences of God and with the teachings of all the great spiritual figures.

So the practice of faith is a continual and deliberate striving to integrate the gift of my experiences and the long human tradition of seeking God with my knowledge and experience of the universe while leaving room for events beyond my ken and beyond verbal expression to have occurred to others. It is a deeply challenging effort to which "practice" in terms of trying to get better at it aptly applies.

---

77. Simcha Jacobovici and Charles Pellegrino, *The Jesus Family Tomb* (San Francisco: HarperSanFrancisco, 2007).

78. Isn't conception and birth through sex miraculous enough?

Chapter 17

The Work of
Keeping the Faith

IT IS DIFFICULT to remain in the Roman Catholic Church as a feminist astronomer. Through the church, the teachings of Jesus and the insights of the saints have been communicated to me. Its teachings along with many of its members, ex-members, and non-members have been woven into my own experiences to form the image and understanding of God I have tried to communicate in these pages. I have known truly good and holy people within the church. And yet it never stops being a challenge to remain within its walls.

As an astronomer, I struggle with what I believe about Jesus and God. It is impossible for me to believe something simply because someone tells me to. Granted, I believe many results in physics and astronomy that I have not personally reproduced, but others have reproduced the results, and I can compare the data and the methods. With scripture, tradition, and religious experience, there are no confirming data. At best, there are hunches and glimmers of truth or untruth that have to be carefully considered and evaluated. The work of faith is taking the time for and making the effort to study, think, discuss, meditate, and pray that this evaluation requires.

I interpret the physical events reported in scripture as metaphor. Scripture was written, selected, and translated by human beings as accurate and trustworthy and inaccurate and untrustworthy as people today. For instance, the oldest Gospel, Mark, begins with Jesus' baptism, Matthew and Luke begin with the foretelling of Jesus' birth, and John, thought to be the most recent of the Gospels begins with "In the beginning was the Word, and the Word was with God, and the Word was God." This progression indicates to some that the idea that Jesus was the son of God and an actual embodiment of God arose in the Christian community after his death and not with Jesus. Scripture scholars struggle to identify what Jesus may have actually said and what the evangelists may have invented since they were interested in communicating spiritual truth, not historical accuracy. Thus, the truth I seek in scripture is truth about God, Jesus, humanity, and the spiritual journey. It is not scripture stories of miracles that convince me of the extraordinariness of Jesus, but the transformation of the Apostles and the fact that we are still discussing, studying, and striving to imitate him millennia later. This is true of a few others in human history: Zoroaster, Confucius, Buddha, and Muhammad among them, but Jesus is the one I know the most about and the one knitted into my culture, my language, and my thinking.

The question about Jesus with which I struggle the most is whether he was different from the rest of us in kind or in degree. Atonement theology, in which Jesus died to atone for the sins of humankind, in particular the sins of Eve and Adam eating the fruit of the tree of knowledge, requires Jesus to be different in kind. This, I believe, is because the many sacrifices of human beings for each other at work, at war, and in childbirth could not atone for sin; it took someone of God's own kin and kind, profoundly different from the rest of us.

This theology did not satisfy me as a child and still makes no sense to me. Humanity has emerged slowly through the processes of evolution. When did humans[79] first wonder about God or sense the whoness of the universe that I sense? It may be impossible for us to know. Do animals sense God? We can't know that either. What we do

---

79. We humans do seem to differ from animals in this, but then, the differences among humans can seem fairly large. I do not know how much animals, particularly the whales who seem to sing epic poems through the corridors of the sea share our sense of God and striving to go beyond mere survival, so though I speak of humans, we may not be alone on this journey. Actually, given the number of stars and galaxies, it's highly *un*-likely we're alone on this journey!

know is that at some point people did start to sense God's presence and begin relating to that presence. Scripture, I believe, is one of the chronicles of people struggling to relate to God and transcend our natures as purely biological creatures focused only on survival. The story of Adam and Eve assumes humans to have been created completely good by a completely good God and attempts to explain how we could become capable of evil. No such explanation is required for biological creatures evolving out of the struggle for survival. Self-preservation is deep in every one of us from the moment of our birth and perhaps even earlier. A perceived threat can quickly bring up very primitive survival instincts. Those instincts, responding to non-existent threats, misdirected, or uncontrolled can lead to great evil, as any reading of newspapers and human history reveals.

The fear of death is also deep in us, and I see this often expressing itself as fear of not mattering or not being important. In fact, there are those who fear not having mattered more than death as evidenced by some suicides. Dying as a martyr with memorial posters and videos can, I imagine, look like less of a death than toiling away in poverty for a lifetime, only to die in obscurity. So human evil is a natural, if miscued or misdirected element of human nature that emerged from evolution with us. We were never completely good and it took no event to make us capable of evil so there's no "fall" for Jesus' death to atone for.

So what does it mean for Christians to say that "Jesus died for our sins"? I have deeply sought the answer to this question. In 2003, I spent thirty days in silence following the Spiritual Exercises of St. Ignatius under the direction of my dear friend, Tom Clarke, S.J., and with the support of his community at Bethany Spirituality Center in Highland Mills, New York. The essence of the retreat was laid out by St. Ignatius in the mid 1500s as a sequence of meditations on scripture. It has been translated and analyzed throughout the centuries and gone through a significant revival in the past few decades, particularly among lay people. Tom had me use David Fleming's text, *Draw Me into Your Friendship* to access Ignatius's words and a modern interpretation of them.[80] Each day has four or five exercises; meditation periods with preparation time and reflection time that generally add up to about an hour and a half for each. There's also a daily conversation with the director, describing thoughts, feelings, and experiences in the exercises. The director combines that information with his or her knowledge of the Spiritual Exercises (Ignatius laid out the Exercises with some flexibility), the retreatant, and his or her own prayerful reflection to discern the meditations for the next day. It's an intense and exhausting experience for both the director and retreatant. Each day I would meet with Tom to discuss what was going on in whatever mood the meditations had brought me to. Sometimes I was joyful, but more often confused, frustrated, sad, or angry. After supper (all meals are taken in silence), I would find a typewritten assignment from Tom, laying out the next day's meditations. Tom's assignment for each day had me focus on a particular grace to seek, the four Ignatian exercises I was to do (they are numbered and explained in the text), and extra notes, clarifications, explanations, and suggestions.

The retreat is broken into "weeks" that do not necessarily correspond to calendar weeks. There are different emphases in the different weeks, but the third week is the darkest. The meditation periods in this week focus on human sin and the passion of Jesus. One spends days meditating on Jesus' journey to Jerusalem, the last supper, the scene in the Garden of Gethsemane where Jesus was betrayed by Judas and his consequent arrest, torture, and death. During this time it is recommended that the retreatant fast from food and, in my case, even from sunlight and the view of the lake from my hermitage. On the first day of the Third Week, after a break day on which I had only an early morning and evening exercise and lunch with the retreat house community, Tom had me seek the grace "to feel grief and contrition that Jesus endured so much suffering out of

---

80. David L. Fleming, S.J., *Draw Me into Your Friendship: A Literal Translation and A Contemporary Reading* (St. Louis: Institute of Jesuit Sources, 1996).

love for me and for my sins."[81] This brought me right up against both my ambivalence toward atonement theology and my inability to see or feel Jesus as anything more than a historical figure.

On the second day of the Third Week, Tom (and Ignatius) had me meditate on Jesus' arrest in Gethsemane and appearance before Annas, the Jewish high priest, before Herod, the king, and finally before Pontius Pilate, the Roman governor. As I discussed my experiences with Tom, he pointed out that none of my descriptions expressed sorrow that my sins had contributed to Jesus' suffering and death. I agreed and replied, "Jesus still isn't *real* to me. The central mystery of Christianity leaves me cold. All the bushes are burning,[82] yet I can't touch Jesus." I spent that evening mostly on the floor of my darkened room, praying mightily for the grace to know Jesus as a real person — the Living Christ that others speak of so easily — and to "feel grief and contrition" for his suffering. I thought back through my life looking for an experience where Jesus had been real to me. The memory of my sexual assault emerged with much pain and anger. I cried out to this Jesus I was seeking that "you weren't with me that night! I had trusted God, Jesus, and the universe — and the universe betrayed me! You weren't there! You don't know what its like to have the universe betray you. I was just a kid! You were in your thirties and had all those mystical experiences and knew you had power. You don't know how it felt." The only response I got from this rant was a still small voice saying, "I do know how it feels to be betrayed."

It wasn't a lightning stroke experience of "the Living Christ." Maybe it was just my own voice answering on Jesus' behalf. I don't know. It did lead me to wonder if Jesus had been raped by the guards who gave him the purple robe and crown of thorns. This connected me with his suffering and the thought that perhaps Jesus suffered

81. Ibid. paraphrased from *Spiritual Exercises*, 193, p. 149 and additional comments from Tom.

82. A reference to Moses' awareness of God's presence in a bush that was burning, yet not consuming itself. I see God so knitted into the universe that all the bushes, trees, rocks, people, animals, and stars are burning.

betrayal, abuse, torture, and death so that twenty centuries later he could say to the clod of Earth[83] that is Aileen, "I know how it feels to be betrayed." More, perhaps he suffered so that he can say it to every clod of Earth.

A new twofold understanding of the idea that "Jesus died for our sins" emerged from this experience. First, Jesus died as a victim of human abuse[84] and none of us can claim to have never abused another, however minimal, unintentional, or unknowing the abuse may have been. Thus all of us have victims and in that way contribute to the victimhood of Jesus. Second, it is also said that "Jesus died so that sins could be forgiven." This is most often taken as meaning that God was somehow unable to forgive human sins until Jesus suffered. This seems an awkward limit of God's power. During that dark evening of my retreat, I realized that only the victim of abuse can actually forgive the abuse. By Jesus' acceptance of human abuse, he became the victim of it and forgave it as a victim. It's important to understand that forgiveness is not forgetfulness. To forgive something does not mean to ignore the harm that was done or act as though it never occurred. Forgiving abuse does not mean justifying or approving it and does not hinder prosecution and punishment for offenders. It does mean for the victims to allow the event to have been in the past and let go of as much of the hurt and rage as they are able. In this letting go, they reduce the power of the abuse to harm the future of their lives as it has harmed their past. Since all of us abuse at some point, in forgiving those who abused him, Jesus forgives every one of us our abuses so that we can stop denying them and beating up ourselves and each other for them. Maybe then we can start getting past all the abuse that continues to propagate through the generations. Because by his death, Jesus displayed the only true way to disempower evil: for those to whom evil is done to not do evil themselves. Only when

---

83. Here I paraphrase Carl Jung, who said, "In my case Pilgrim's Progress consisted in my having to climb down a thousand ladders until I could reach out my hand to the little clod of earth that I am."

84. During my thirty days of silence I came to understand sin almost exclusively as abuse. Abuse of each other, ourselves, other creatures, and the Earth itself.

people don't abuse back and don't abuse forward[85] can the propagation of abuse be reduced. That is what Jesus did and he did so as a teacher, a prophet, a friend and even a son of God.

In his book, *Violence Unveiled*, Gil Bailie argues that Jesus' teachings and death taught us a sympathy for the victim unknown in the ancient world, where illness, poverty, and misfortune were taken as God's disfavor due to sin.[86] Job struggles with being the innocent victim. Jesus teaches us compassion for the victim. In the centuries since Jesus, compassion for the victim has increased — by fits and starts with many backslides — but increased nonetheless. For all our failures to actually help the victims of war, abuse, and economic and natural disasters, there are seldom, if ever, arguments that we should not help. We do still find ways to blame the victims, and I find it tragic that some do it in the name of Christ, but Bailie argues that humanity is much more compassionate toward victims than it would have been without Jesus.

My faith in Jesus, in Christ, then, rests in his teaching of peace, concern for the poor, and forgiveness coupled with whatever happened to his disciples that so profoundly changed them. Was he the son of God, different from us in kind? Or was he different from us simply in degree so that all of us can aspire to become Christs as Buddhists can aspire to becoming Buddhas? I don't know the answer to this, and all I can do is "rest in unknowing" since the answer has no bearing on my faith or my practice.

The difficulty of believing the tenets of the Catholic Church as a scientist aside, there is another, greater difficulty in my continued participation the church. Some of my peers react with surprise to find out that I'm a practicing Catholic. Some women have reacted with outright hostility that I "enable" such a dysfunctional, misogynist, hierarchical institution by staying in the pews. Even within myself I can feel that I betray women, or even all of humanity, by staying. So

---

85. Again, this does not exclude punishing offenders!
86. Gil Bailie, *Violence Unveiled: Humanity at the Crossroads* (New York: Crossroad, 1995).

why do I stay? That's a question I ask myself constantly and there may come a day when I don't stay, but so far that day has not arrived.

The practical reason I stay is because in the rituals, prayers, singing, and silences, I sometimes feel immersed in the whoness, immersed in God. I feel such immersion at other times, as well, such as when I lay beneath the two-hundred-inch telescope at Palomar bathed in the ancient light of galaxies or when I stood nude in a cleansing, healing rain after a week in the hospital. But somehow, in a darkened church before Mass, in silent prayer with other seekers, I can more easily attune my spirit to the touch of God, so hard to perceive in the rush of daily life.

The deeper reason I stay is that I bump into extraordinary, deeply spiritual people who are also sticking it out with the church in spite of its profound flaws. These people are rare, even within the church, and certainly exist outside the church, but there are just enough of them inside the church to keep me lurking in its pews seeking spiritual companions and guides. What they invite me into when I find them is the "Great Tradition" that transcends the tenets of the catechism. It is the tradition of the true spiritual journey lived and expressed by mystics and saints through the centuries. It's the tradition that Augustine spoke from when he said "Love and do what you will," knowing that love — real, deeply generous love, not the pseudolove seeking possession that leads to much violence — does not need rules as it seeks the benefit of the other. The great tradition is where the Dalai Lama and Thomas Merton met and knew each other as brothers. The differences in their religions, profound as they are, are window dressing to the great tradition. In my staying in the church, I seek to learn and grow from the great tradition. It was the great tradition that fostered mystics such as St. Francis and Teilhard de Chardin that called me to San Miguel Church to begin this strange journey of faith.

The person who led me most deeply into the great tradition was Tom Clarke. I first met him when a friend suggested I go on an eight-day silent retreat at Wadhams Hall, a seminary-college in

Ogdensburg. Catherine told me that Tom was a Jesuit. I have always been attracted to the intellectual tradition of the Jesuits but had not had an opportunity to get to know any Jesuits simply because they weren't in Aurora, Socorro, or northern New York. I accepted Catherine's suggestion and signed up for the retreat.

A month before the retreat I collapsed from anemia due to a bleeding ulcer I hadn't known I had. There were no symptoms until I suddenly couldn't stand up without my heart racing and my head swimming accompanied by nausea and a cold sweat. My friend, Ann, took me to the ER,[87] where I was admitted for transfusions and a week of tests. In spite of having been out of the hospital for three weeks before the retreat, I was still exhausted from the entire ordeal and asked to commute to the retreat instead of taking up residence at the seminary. Then I met Tom.

A directed retreat is where the retreatants are in silence, breaking it only once a day to talk with a spiritual director. The first day or two are mostly spent catching up on rest and figuring out what to concentrate on. For the first two days I just floundered around, struggling with boredom and listlessness due to my illness. On Tuesday, though, I started talking about how uncomfortable the seminary made me. I complained to Tom that I hated having to walk by the portraits of all the pious bishops of Ogdensburg that hung in the main corridor outside his rooms. I realized that the major reason I was commuting was because the seminary was a repulsive and unwelcoming symbol of the sexist hierarchy of the church. Realizing that, like Job going out to sit in the ash-heap, I moved to my room at Wadhams to see if I could face up to some of my anger at the sexist, hierarchical church.

In my meditations and prayers (some quite tearful) and in my talks with Tom, an incredible synthesis of wounds and anger around gender and abuse took place. Tom sparked this in one of our early meetings where we were discussing my illness and healing. In talking

---

87. Actually, she convinced me to go to the ER as it hadn't crossed my mind until we spoke on the phone.

about healing, he mentioned that people have to want to be healed and that there is often resistance to healing. Now this was not a new idea to me, but it was the first time that I seriously asked if I resisted healing. When I was in the hospital I didn't particularly want to go home. The night the anemia had me collapsing on the floor scared me, and I didn't want to be responsible for my own health again. I had been wondering if I was milking my illness a bit out of a desire for the nurturing it gained me. I didn't know if I did, but the important wound turned out to be more spiritual and emotional than physical.

The wound that I resisted healing was that of sexism and my deep pain and anger over it. In the course of our discussions, in the context of discussing my illness, I was telling Tom about my conversion to Catholicism from atheism in graduate school due to despair over my fear of death and meaninglessness. I described my sexual assault to him as one of the roots of my fear. What I found myself saying to Tom, to my own surprise, was that I felt that the hand of the church, our sexist, hierarchical Church of Rome, helped hold the gun to my head by its sanction, defense, and even *blessing* of the cultural devaluation of women to objects of temptation and procreation.

Rape is a crime of power, not of sex. One of the arguments as to why rape didn't carry much of a penalty for the perpetrator but shamed the victim until very recently (and does to this very day in much of the world) is that rape is a tool of the patriarchy. As long as the fear of rape keeps women in need (real or imagined) of the protection of males, it feeds power to the males. The church has fed power to males by excluding women from its primary ministry of priesthood. When I led retreats for the women's community at Manna House in Kansas, we could not celebrate Mass in the community of our retreat, but were forced to go to the local parish for Mass with no connection to the subject or tone of the retreat. The church prevents its women from being complete in their communities by forcing them to always have an outsider offer the sacraments. It's an imposed need for males that has long informed our culture that women need men to help them, to govern them, to make them complete. The way this has informed the culture has resulted in some men needing to subjugate and abuse women to assure themselves that they are "real men." One of those men put a gun to my head. The hand of the church's sexism and hierarchy was also on that gun in its refusal to accept women as equals in seeking, following, and imaging Christ. This hand remains on many guns that terrorize, maim, and murder the children of God, the Body of Christ every hour of every day.

As I reflected on my resistance to allowing the sexism to stop wounding me, my inability to let go of the burning anger, I realized that I did so out of fear that in accepting healing of the wound, I also accepted the sexist hierarchy, and in that I would truly betray my sisters — and my brothers who need equality with women.

I have struggled mightily with whether I betray my sisters by staying in the church and have been vehemently informed that I do by some of them. From my experience of the good people I've known within it and by my experience of the great tradition, though, I also fear I betray my sisters *and* my brothers by abandoning the great tradition to the sexist hierarchy. I don't believe that the current structure of the church is the vision of Christ or God, but mostly the cultural entanglements and power structures of medieval Europe. Those structures actually betray the spirit and ideals on which the church was founded. It is a profoundly flawed institution. And yet it has helped nurture this feminist astronomer's spiritual journey.

As I reflected on being caught between betraying my sisters by staying and by leaving and feeling quite stuck, I recalled a passage from *Zen and the Art of Motorcycle Maintenance* about being caught in a dilemma.[88] I checked out a library copy to read about *stuckness*. In his discussion, Pirsig points out that the screw with the stripped slot holding the cover on the slide cover plate and preventing the mechanic from fixing the motorcycle stops being a screw and becomes the equivalent of the entire motorcycle. The mechanic, faced

---

88. Robert Pirsig, *Zen and the Art of Motorcycle Maintenance* (New York: Bantam, 1981), 250–58.

with this changed view of the universe and the failure of reason, is truly stuck. Have I let the screw-with-the-stripped-slot of the sexist hierarchy become the equivalent of the entire motorcycle of the "one holy, catholic, and apostolic Church"[89] that Catholics proclaim belief in at every Sunday Mass? I certainly feel stuck as I have faced this pain and envy and anger for many years.

I thought that if I could just sit with my wound, just "be" in my stuckness, I might be able to hear the voice of God whispering a word of enlightenment. So I sat. And I wept. In my evening prayer (from *The Celtic Devotional*)[90] the topic for meditation was "the complementarity of men and women." In that meditation I realized that though I love both maleness and femaleness, the masculine and the feminine, and their differences, I am terrified to admit the differences because they have been used for so long to make what is female, feminine, and me, less than what is male, masculine, and "the image of Christ" as priest.

I went down to the chapel in the middle of the night. It's a beautiful hexagonal chapel quite incongruous with my view of the seminary as the brick symbol of the hierarchy. I knelt in prayer, offering God my pain and stuckness and asking for wisdom. I sat in the pew and wept. After kneeling and sitting, praying and weeping, I ran out of tears, tissues, and energy.

I slept only a few hours and was up again at 4:30 a.m., sitting with coffee, looking northwest out the window of my room across the St. Lawrence River at the sky brightening over Canada. In the prayer from the *Celtic Devotional*, the meditation question was "Who do I need to forgive the most?" As I meditated and prayed, I realized that it was myself in my own internalization of sexism that I needed to forgive the most.

---

89. The "catholic" in the Nicene creed, it should be noted, has a lower-case c, not a capital C. It is the truly catholic, that is, universal church, not the Roman Catholic Church.

90. Caitlin Matthews, *Celtic Devotional* (New York: Harmony Books, 1996).

It's the internalization of sexism that made me accept the judg-ment that I am less than my brothers, that the pious bishops have power over me, and that my body, in its femaleness, is something to hate. It started very early on, when my brothers would put me down for being "just a girl." I wanted to be a boy. I felt like a boy. I hung out with boys — climbed trees, built forts, caught frogs, and pre-tended I wasn't a girl. I despised girls, particularly "good girls" whose presence would usually get me reprimanded for not being like them. They represented the confining box I was supposed to fit. My image of that box was that of the medieval executioners' coffins with spikes on the lid that would impale and kill the person when the coffin was closed. I distanced myself from being a girl by despising them — as some women do throughout their lives. (I believe I hear the echo of this in some women's demonization of feminists.) The greatest com-pliment from my early childhood friends was that I didn't act like a girl. My mother still recalls that when accused of hanging out with a girl, my friends Danny and David would reply, "That's not a girl, that's Aileen." From my earliest years, I was *good* at being a boy. I was terrible at being a girl. Every time I had to "act like a lady" I ended up being uncomfortable, bored, and reprimanded a lot. When people remembered that I was a girl, my freedom would be curtailed and I'd be corralled in the house or yard, while the boys went on roaming free. Who would want to be a girl? When my breasts developed I felt betrayed by my body. When my period started, I felt punished by it. This was all made much worse by being sexually assaulted.

The assault happened to me in eighth grade, when I was starting to make some peace with actually being a girl. It plunged me into a deeper hatred for my body than I had ever known before. I found my body repulsive and filthy after I was assaulted — as though my own body was responsible for assaulting me instead of a man! That hatred of my body has not completely gone away. My fear of betraying my sisters lies, I think, in fear of my internalized sexism and its exposure. It lies in my fear of being found to be in "collaboration with the enemy" due to the sexism of my culture and my church having been knitted as deeply into me as my native language. It is probably within us all in ways we don't even recognize; in our cultural values and expressions and those reactions that feel like instinct or intuition. In some it flips to a devaluation of everything masculine, but that is still the same coin of sexism. Sexism is *not* men against women as some would paint it; it is all of us having subconscious values and attitudes from the patriarchal roots and currents of our culture that values the attributes of maleness over those of femaleness.

I shared the passage on stuckness in Pirsig with Tom. He gave me a copy of *Impasse and Dark Night,* an essay by Constance FitzGerald, O.C.D.[91] In this essay, she equates an impasse as the "dark night" of St. John of the Cross in much the same way that Pirsig defines stuckness. "In a true impasse, every normal manner of acting is brought to a standstill, and ironically, impasse is experienced not only in the problem itself but also in any solution rationally attempted." She goes on to argue that we who see sexism as evil are truly stuck; we are at an impasse:

> The feminists see a patriarchal system that visualizes God, and consequently church, in almost exclusively patriarchal terms as basically destructive. The masculine image of God is experienced as unsatisfying and confusing because it serves to reinforce male domination, a patriarchal values system, and an entire male world view.
>
> This is an impasse for women, since their past religious experience has come to them through these images and this inherited symbol system, which does not function for women now as it did before. There is no going back to what was — what gave comfort and clarity and brought feminists to their present stage of religious development and commitment — but there is no satisfactory going forward either.

91. *In Women's Spirituality,* ed. Joann Wolski Conn (Mahwah, NJ: Paulist Press, 1986).

Pirsig finds stuckness a positive thing: "It's exactly this stuckness that Zen Buddhists go to so much trouble to induce; through koans, deep breathing, sitting still, and the like. Your mind is empty, you have a 'hollow-flexible' attitude of 'beginner's mind.'" Both Pirsig and Fitz-Gerald conclude that the only available option is to stay stuck in the dark night and allow the non-rational mind to find or create a solution. FitzGerald says, "The only way to break out . . . is to surrender in faith and trust to the unfathomable" because "it is the experience . . . that is transforming the human person." Pirsig states that "stuckness shouldn't be avoided. It is the predecessor of all real understanding. An egoless acceptance of stuckness is a key to an understanding of all Quality in mechanical work as in other endeavors." Hence the impasse of the sexism of the church is filled with potential:

> *If* the impasse in which feminists find themselves *is* dark night, then a new experience of God, transformative of alienating symbols, is already breaking through even though it is not comprehensible yet, and impasse is a call to development, transcendence, new life, and understanding. . . . What is critical to see is that one has to allow the experience to take place through a love that is gradually welling up from the ground of one's being and that serves as a basis for contemplation. . . . How imperative it is that women take possession of their pain and confusion; actively appropriate their experience of domination, exploitation, and oppression; consent to their time in history; and hold this impasse in their bodies and their hearts before the inner God they reach for in the dark of shattered symbols. [italics FitzGerald's]

My work of keeping the faith is in struggling to be patient in my stuckness with the church even as I strive to eliminate the nagging dislike of myself arising from my internalized sexism. At the end of the retreat, I asked Tom for both the physical and psychic sacraments of healing. I confessed the corporate sin of the sexism of the church and culture as a member of both guilty of the sin. It was the first time I discussed anything about the church in confession as an insider, addressing the church as "we" instead of an outsider for whom the church is "they." At last I may have learned what Pogo knew: "We have met the enemy and they are us."[92] I asked for forgiveness and healing of this wound in me, and in doing so, forgave the church so that it would not have the power to injure me further. That way, when my sisters (and brothers) struggle with the same wound, perhaps I can be strong and wise enough to be of some help.

It is impossible to express the profound respect and compassion I felt from Tom during this and consequent spiritual journeys. As one who had lived within and been a part of the church's structures and hierarchy, he accepted my anger and pain with tenderness and not the least hint of defensiveness. He saw the church's profound flaws, too. After this intense journey, the pious bishops in the hallway did not offend me as I walked by them.

My anger and pain at the church's sexism, deepened now by the bishops' cover-ups and enabling of sexual abuse of children, has not gone away and can certainly flame up. But it does not have the intensity and power it had before that first retreat with Tom.

My struggle with whether staying in the church or leaving it betrays women more also continues. For now I remain in the church but insist on speaking of my own experience of God, my understanding of the universe, and my interpretation of the Gospels and teachings of Christ whether or not they align with the church's current teachings.

A friend in the throes of leaving the church because she feels she can no longer enable the dysfunctional institution asked me how I can go to Communion with all my disagreements with the church. I responded that I am fully in communion with every true seeker of

---

92. On an Earth Day poster in 1970 and a comic strip in 1971, Walt Kelly's comic strip character Pogo states, "We have met the enemy and he is us," paraphrasing U.S. Navy Commodore Oliver Hazard Perry's "We have met the enemy and he is ours" in 1813. See *www.en.wikipedia.org/wiki/Pogo.*

the great tradition, of spiritual wisdom, of the full integration of their spiritual and physical selves, and of the universe.

As the Dalai Lama said, we have to believe there is one path and one truth at the same time we believe that there are many paths and many truths. My path has been jagged and my truth elusive. I hope that this description of it will help you, dear reader, make a step or two along your path — or at least make peace with some of its twists!